YACHTING MONTHLY

COMPUTERS ON BOARD

TIM THORNTON

ADLARD COLES NAUTICAL
LONDON

*To Cath, for reminding me
of wider horizons.*

Published by Adlard Coles Nautical
an imprint of A & C Black Publishers Ltd
38 Soho Square, London, W1D 3HB
www.adlardcoles.com

Copyright © Tim Thornton 2007

First edition 2007

ISBN 978-0-7136-8354-7

All rights reserved. No part of this publication may be reproduced in any form or by any means – graphic, electronic or mechanical, including photocopying, recording, taping or information storage and retrieval systems – without the prior permission in writing of the publishers.

The right of the author to be identified as the author of this work has been asserted by him in accordance with the Copyright, Designs and Patents Act, 1988.

A CIP catalogue record for this book is available
from the British Library.

This book is produced using paper that is made from wood grown in managed, sustainable forests. It is natural, renewable and recyclable. The logging and manufacturing processes conform to the environmental regulations of the country of origin.

Set in 10/14pt Syntax by
Falcon Oast Graphic Art Ltd.

Printed and bound in Spain by Graphy Gems

Note: while all reasonable care has been taken in the publication of this book, the publisher takes no responsibility for the use of the methods or products described in the book.

CONTENTS

Introduction	1
Hardware Decisions	2
Keeping in Touch	14
Connecting to the Internet	24
Comms Configuration	35
Weather or Not to Sail?	51
Navigation	62
Entertainment	83
Putting it All Together	89
Over the Horizon	97
Shutdown	101
Jargon Buster	103
Index	107

INTRODUCTION

Having a computer on board is now a commonplace affair, though different people use it in different ways. Even 5 years ago it was seen as a bit unusual to have one on board, and it was still the preserve of higher-end race boats, long distance cruisers needing e-mail communications, and techno-geeks enjoying using leading-edge technology. Now, nobody blinks an eye at the use of a computer on board, with many users on 2nd or 3rd generation systems. Hardware has become relatively cheap, and software providers are moving on from being leading edge, technically driven start-up companies, to more mature organisations concentrating on producing software to meet the customer's need for a stable, reliable system.

Navigation, weather, communications, entertainment: these are all areas in which a computer can be used. We will be looking at all of these aspects in this book, starting off with hardware considerations.

A general knowledge of PCs and Windows is assumed – for more basic information on using a PC, there are many introductory books. We will be concentrating on specifically marine aspects, whether it is a way of setting up your computer that is different from use at home or in the office, or a specific marine application. Marine applications for Macs and Linux are virtually non-existent compared with the range for the Windows platform, and won't be covered in this book.

You can either read through the book from cover to cover for a comprehensive overview, or you can dip in and out of the chapters to extract information as you need it. At the end of each chapter, you will find a list of any relevant suppliers and organisations and their websites. And at the back of the book, there's a 'jargon buster' section, giving brief definitions for any jargon used.

COMPUTERS ON BOARD

HARDWARE DECISIONS

Before getting too involved in the various applications, in this first chapter let's first look at the hardware side of things. What you need, how to install it, and power and interfacing considerations.

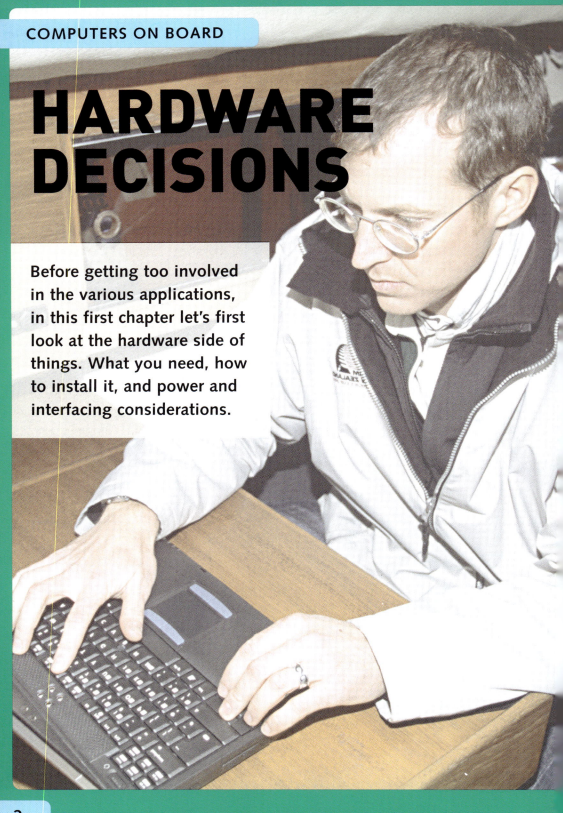

HARDWARE DECISIONS

PERFORMANCE

The performance you need depends on what you want to use the computer for. If you want it for e-mail and web browsing, and for basic navigation software, then any new PC you can buy at the moment is more than powerful enough in terms of processor power, memory and disk capacity. In fact, there are arguments for choosing a lower specification computer, to save power and space on board.

The performance you need depends on what you want to use the computer for

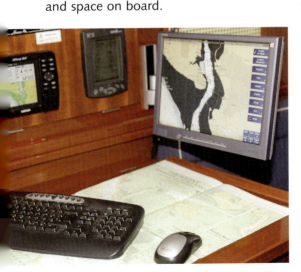

A neat installation at the chart table: the screen swings out of the way when not needed, and the cordless keyboard and mouse drop into a drawer.

If you want to use the computer for graphics-intensive applications, such as radar or 3D views in the chart plotter, video editing or even 3D computer games, then you will want a high performance CPU (possibly a dual processor model), and as much memory (RAM) as you can install – 1 or 2GB. A high-performance graphics processor is also a big benefit, though this is one area where laptops lose out to a fixed PC. A more powerful computer will also be more future proof, as new versions of Windows and new application software will inevitably require more power, so the faster the computer you buy now, the longer it will be until it needs upgrading on performance grounds.

Of the current ranges of processors, in terms of performance the entry level CPUs are AMD's Athlon 64 series. Next in speed are Intel's Pentium 4 series and the Athlon FX series. Then we get on to the latest dual core technologies, starting with AMD's Athlon X2, then Pentium 4D and EE, and Intel Core 2 at the top. There is some overlap in these different series, depending on the clock speeds, but this is a good general guide.

Memory is at least as important as processor speed these days, as otherwise Windows will always be swapping things in and out to your hard disk. 512MB should be seen as a minimum specification, and with memory being so cheap these days it doesn't cost much more to go up to 2GB.

Disk size is generally not an issue,

COMPUTERS ON BOARD

unless you want to use the computer for video editing, or you have a very large collection of sound files and digital camera images that you want to keep on your computer.

Measuring computer performance has become ever more complex, with an increasing range of processor families. Some of these are better for graphics; others are more suitable for number crunching, and the ever more complex interaction with the other components of the computer. If you want to delve into this further, a good starting point is www.tomshardware.com.

DISPLAY

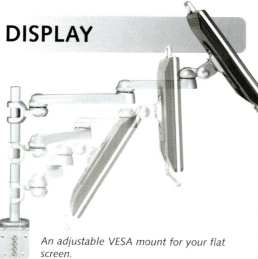

An adjustable VESA mount for your flat screen.

For the display, the larger and higher resolution it is the better, though this obviously has both space and power implications – the screen is one of the biggest power consumers on a laptop. Many displays now come in a widescreen format, which is ideal for playing DVDs, but be aware that some chart plotting software gives a distorted view when used with these screens, as it has been written to support the original 4:3 screen aspect ratio, instead of the new 16:9 wide format.

If you are using a fixed computer, or an external display attached to your laptop, you will typically have a screen mounted at the chart table. Just about all screens can have their bases taken off for mounting flat against a bulkhead, or on a swivel arm if you want to be able to swing it over to the saloon. There is a standard VESA mount specification, which specifies the size and location of mounting holes. Most screens comply with this standard, and there is a wide variety of mounting brackets designed for VESA mounts.

The larger and higher resolution the display is, the better

If you want to have a display in the cockpit, you need something that is both waterproof and significantly brighter than a standard display. The problem is that sunlight viewable screens generate a lot of heat, and it is difficult to engineer a waterproof screen that can cope with the thermal variations without overheating or letting in moisture. I would recommend going to a specialist manufacturer, such as KS Bootronik, to ensure you have a reliable unit. An alternative approach is to have a small handheld touch display, connected to your computer by Wi-Fi or Bluetooth.

HARDWARE DECISIONS

Panasonic do a small Wi-Fi touch screen that repeats whatever is on your computer screen, and is waterproof enough to use in a protected environment on deck. Some PDAs also have software available that lets them act as repeaters for your computer screen, though the lower resolution of the PDA screen means that either the resolution is reduced significantly, or you need to pan around to see a bit of the screen at a time, which means that this isn't really suited to more than occasional use.

As far as the operating system is concerned, the only choice is between Windows XP and Windows Vista. For use on board, there are no significant differences between XP Home and Professional. However, if you plan to use your computer for entertainment, there are benefits in the Media Centre edition, and there is more information on this in the entertainment chapter.

LAPTOP OR FIXED PC?

A fixed PC comes into its own as part of a more complex system

For the majority of users, a laptop offers the flexibility of being able to use the computer off as well as on the boat, whether it is to prepare for your next cruise, or to use in the office. Whilst there are ruggedised laptops, like the Panasonic Toughbooks, you do pay a significant price and performance

A laptop built into a locker, making it secure and protected when not in use.

COMPUTERS ON BOARD

penalty, and for most cruising yachts the environment does not warrant this if the laptop is properly installed.

If you intend to use it at sea, I would strongly advise against putting the laptop onto the chart table. You lose the use of the chart table, and sooner or later the laptop will get damaged. A much better solution is to locate the laptop in a locker and connect it to a display mounted at the chart table, with a cordless keyboard and mouse that can both be dropped into a drawer when not in use. The laptop is protected, the chart table is clear, and all the wiring is neatly out of the way. If a wave comes down the hatch, or somebody grabs hold of the screen and damages it, you still have the laptop intact.

A fixed PC comes into its own as part of a more complex system where the computer is interfaced to more equipment and you want the ultimate performance. Or, on a larger boat with more than one computer, you can use a fixed PC as the hub of the system, with other PCs or laptops elsewhere on the boat. A fixed PC also has the benefit that it can be upgraded over time, whereas with a laptop the only real option is to replace it.

As with laptops, fixed PCs can either be standard desktops, like the compact Shuttle range, or the even smaller Corretto from WSPC, or they can be more rugged units based on industrial PC components. The latter are more expensive, but will last significantly longer, with a greater tolerance of humidity, temperature and vibration, and often a wider range of case sizes and options. Hard disks are generally shock-mounted inside the case; components are positively secured rather than relying on gravity; cooling air is filtered and pumped through faster; DC power supplies are available as well as AC; and the case is generally more robust.

Digital Yacht's package of computer, screen, keyboard and mouse, ready to install on your boat.

On many industrial PCs, the standard motherboard is replaced with a passive backplane, so the processor is on a standard plug-in board that can easily be removed for maintenance or repair. The downsides of these PCs are that they tend to be noisier (due to the fan and extra cooling) and the latest – and fastest – technology takes a little while to appear.

Putting aside any technical issues, if you will be doing any extended cruising, you need to look at the warranty and after-sales support. If you are cruising around the Mediterranean and have a computer problem, it is much easier to get the manufacturer to pick up and return the PC than it is to have to ship it back to the UK for repair. Some manufacturers and insurance companies offer insurance, which will provide cover for accidental damage, shipping costs, and all those other things not offered by a warranty.

REMOTE DISPLAYS

You may have one computer on board, but want to access it from another location – perhaps from a waterproof screen in the cockpit, or a flat screen TV in the saloon, or from a cabin. This requires a KVM (Keyboard, Video, Monitor) switch, which lets you attach multiple displays, keyboards and mice to one computer (or access multiple computers from one location). This is an area where it pays to invest in good quality cabling and components, or the remote screens will look fuzzy and suffer from

COMPUTERS ON BOARD

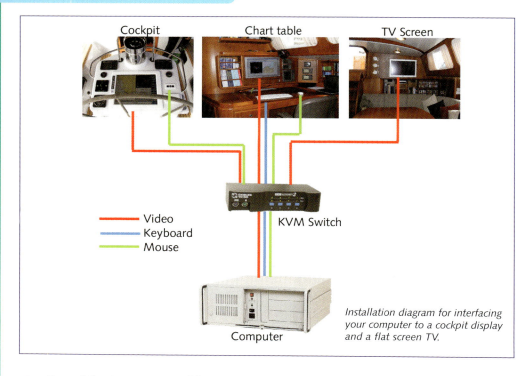

Installation diagram for interfacing your computer to a cockpit display and a flat screen TV.

ghosting of the image. For cable runs of up to about 10m, you can use good quality video and PS/2 cabling. Above this, it pays to switch to a system that uses CAT5 cabling, to ensure that quality is maintained. Note that, although this is the same cabling as is used on a network, the connection is not a network one, and the cabling needs to be separate from any network cabling you may have installed.

MULTIPLE COMPUTERS

Even leaving aside superyachts, it is not uncommon for yachts to carry more than one computer these days. The most common scenario is to have a built-in 'ship's computer', augmented by a laptop that is brought on and off the boat as required. It makes sense to network these computers together, to enable the sharing of files, printers, e-mail and Internet connections. This can be done using either Wi-Fi or network cabling – cabling is more reliable, and should be used for fixed PCs, but Wi-Fi gives you flexibility if you are using a laptop. If using Wi-Fi, the best approach is to fit a wireless access point on board, to act as a hub for any laptops or other Wi-Fi devices you may have on board. This on-board Wi-Fi network has to be kept separate from any Wi-Fi network you use at the marina, and to get the best

HARDWARE DECISIONS

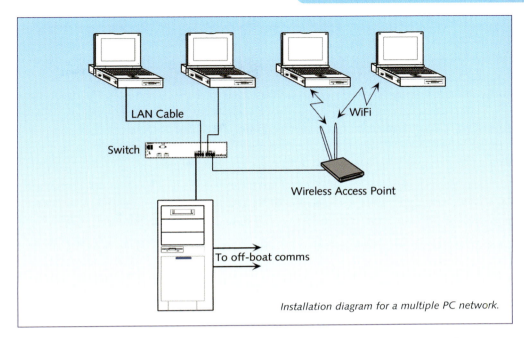

Installation diagram for a multiple PC network.

performance you should ensure that, when the two networks are in use at the same time, they use different channels, thereby avoiding interference.

POWER CONSIDERATIONS

There are two aspects to power: the source of power, and adjusting the computer to minimise power consumption.

Your Computer's Power Supply

In general, computers and displays are designed to be powered from mains electricity, and this is best provided by a pure sine wave inverter. Modified sine wave inverters can result in interference or other problems with some computer kit, though some are better than others. A 300W inverter is usually large enough to cover peak demands, but with larger screens and faster processors, it may now be worth going up to 500W; the average consumption is considerably less. Some laptops have an optional 12V or car adaptor, normally with a cigarette lighter socket, which is more efficient than an inverter, and some accessory manufacturers (such as Targus) also produce car adaptors. Industrial PC-based units are often supplied with a 12V or 24V DC power supply, and these can cope with a wide range of voltages.

COMPUTERS ON BOARD

Do not try to plug your screen or laptop direct into the boat's DC supply. Even if the output of the mains power supply is 12V DC, the computer expects a regulated supply. The DC supply on your boat will vary greatly, from 9 or 10V when the batteries are nearly dead, to 17 or 18V when they are being fast charged. This is likely to cause your computer to power off in the first instance, and blow up in the second!

Minimising Power Consumption

The easiest way of minimising the power consumed by your computer is to avoid too high a specification. The table below gives an indication of the power consumed by the key components of a computer: CPU, graphics processor, memory, hard disk and display. The left hand column shows full power, worst case scenarios; the right hand column shows how the power consumption is reduced when idle, or when memory saving features are implemented. Note that this table does not include start-up power requirements when, for example, a hard disk may draw 30W as it spins up to speed.

Item	Full load power (W)	Light load power (W)
CPU	20–150	8–60 (idle with power saving on)
Graphics processor	24–120	12–29
RAM (DDR2, 2GB)	11	4
Hard disk	9–15	5–9
15in TFT	21–50	0–5 (standby)
Power supply	17–120	6–37
Total	102–466	35–144

Looking at this table, it is obvious that the CPU can easily be the biggest power drain, but there is a large variation in power consumption. As may be expected, the faster the processor, the more power it generally draws. The newer processor technologies tend to draw less power than older ones of the same processing power, due to improvements in design giving a lower processor speed for a given processing power. Also, low power processors such as those used in Intel's Centrino laptop technology save significant amounts of power.

Another important factor is the graphics processor, where the high end, 3D graphics cards fitted to some desktop machines can consume significant amounts of power.

HARDWARE DECISIONS

It is worth bearing in mind that for marine applications, there is little benefit in having a high specification graphics processor.

The power supply figures are a bit misleading at first sight. The power supply will operate at between 65% and 80% efficiency, so the bigger the overall power drain, the bigger the power loss from the CPU.

With the computer consuming about a third of its power when idle, and allowing for a fairly generous 2 hours a day of hard usage and 8 hours at idle (remembering that we are meant to be sailing, not working at the computer!), the average power consumption is just 20W for an entry-level machine (a daily consumption of 40Ah at 12V DC), comparable to the daily draw from your boat's fridge.

You can have a significant effect on the average power consumption of your computer if you set things up right

You can have a significant effect on the average power consumption of your computer if you set things up right, using the Power Options settings in Control Panel. On any PC, you can use the power saving settings to shut down the screen and the hard disk after a few minutes of not being used. Depending on the computer, you may also be able to reduce the brightness of the screen, slow the processor down, and disable any interfaces you aren't using. If you are using a remote screen on a laptop, make sure that the laptop's own screen is disabled, rather than duplicating what is on the remote screen.

INTERFACING

Many items still use serial ports, which are absent on almost all laptops (though still found on some fixed PCs). The way round this is to use USB to serial converters, which you can get from companies like Maplins or B&B Electronics. USB ports are also used for many other devices such as printers and cameras. If you run out of USB ports, you can use a USB hub to add additional ports.

USB to serial port converter.

Another issue to consider is that the USB specification is designed to buffer data

COMPUTERS ON BOARD

in the interests of efficiency, and this can upset the timing of COM ports. If you have a USB hub, then this also does its own buffering, and further exacerbates the situation.

The result of this is that the computer may not be able to talk to the device at the other end of the USB to serial adaptor. (This is more likely to be an issue with communications devices, as the handshaking and flow control is more complex than with NMEA devices.) A few USB to serial adaptor drivers allow you to configure how frequently the buffer is emptied, and increasing the frequency at which this occurs will help. Alternatively, if you go into the advanced settings for your serial port, you can minimise the buffer size, which has a similar effect.

> ### PLUGGING AND UNPLUGGING USB PORTS
>
> Note that Windows can renumber USB serial ports when they are unplugged and plugged in again whilst the computer is running, or if devices are switched between different USB ports. This is a nuisance, as you will then either need to change the COM port settings in your software, or go into Device Manager, show the old hidden devices and delete them, before going into the COM port settings to renumber the new COM ports to their predecessor's settings. The way round this is to play safe, and only plug and unplug the devices when the computer is switched off, and ensure that you always plug the same device into the same port.

USB and RS232 serial cabling is limited in the length it can be run – 3m for standard USB cables, and 15m for good quality serial cable at the slow data rates used on yachts. There are other options, though. First, a serial network adaptor lets you connect the serial device to your network, and software on the PC makes it look like a normal serial port. This also makes it easy to reallocate devices between computers, without the need for rewiring. Alternatively, for wireless connections, you can get Wi-Fi or Bluetooth serial adaptors.

Other interfaces are used for specific things, such as Bluetooth, Firewire (or IEEE1394), PC Card (or PCMCIA), Wi-Fi and RJ45 network ports, plus audio, video and PS/2 ports. These will all be discussed at the relevant points in the forthcoming chapters.

HARDWARE DECISIONS

USEFUL WEB SITES

B&B Electronics – www.bb-europe.com
Intel – www.intel.com
KS Bootronik – www.bootronik.de
Maplins – www.maplins.co.uk
Microsoft – www.microsoft.com

Panasonic Toughbook – www.toughbook-europe.com
Shuttle – www.shuttle.com
Targus – www.targus.com/uk/
WSPC – www.worldssmallestpc.com

COMPUTERS ON BOARD

KEEPING IN TOUCH

Many people could not spend the amount of time they do on board if mobile communications had not developed as much as they have – but the choice of technology is wide and often confusing. In this chapter we will look at hardware and services, with particular emphasis on voice communications. The following chapter will extend this to cover e-mail and web access.

COMMUNICATIONS ZONES

We can classify communications into three zones: harbour, coastal and offshore. Although offshore communications can be used in coastal waters, and any communications can be used in harbour, this is not always cost effective.

KEEPING IN TOUCH

Harbour

Looking at communications that can only be used in harbour, we have a choice of a standard BT-style land phone line and VoIP (Voice over IP) over a broadband connection, whether a landline or Wi-Fi. There is also Inmarsat's BGAN, which, although it offers coverage over the oceans, at the moment has no marine units with the necessary stabilised antennas for use at sea.

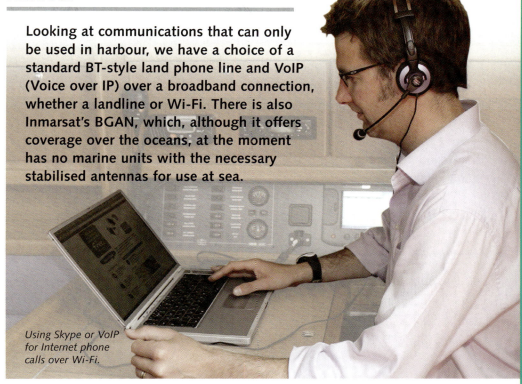

Using Skype or VoIP for Internet phone calls over Wi-Fi.

A landline can be run by BT to your berth in exactly the same way as it can be run to your house. So, if you have a permanent marina berth (and the marina doesn't object), this is well worth considering, although many marinas geared towards larger boats offer a landline facility (though these are mostly abroad). Of course, once you have a landline, you can usually very easily add broadband to it. I think it is safe to assume that there is no need to go into detail on the use of a BT phone line!

For Wi-Fi, you are dependent upon there being a Wi-Fi operator in the marina. This may be provided by the marina themselves, or by a third party provider such as Square Mile. Each operator works independently, so if you sail over to another marina with a different Wi-Fi operator, you will need to pay them for use of their service, on top of any ongoing subscription with the Wi-Fi

If you sail to another marina with a different Wi-Fi operator, you will need to pay them

15

COMPUTERS ON BOARD

provider in your home marina. With Wi-Fi, you need to be aware that the range with a clear path is only 100m, and if the signal is weak the speed is automatically throttled back to make the signal more robust. Reception can be patchy using Wi-Fi built in to a laptop down below: built-in Wi-Fi is not as sensitive, and you are using it close to the water level, often blocked by the marina pontoons.

A better bet is to have an external Wi-Fi unit, hooked up to a Wi-Fi antenna on deck. This will give a significantly faster, more robust connection in most cases.

At present, 'coastal communications' means one thing: mobile phones

Unfortunately, in some locations, the Wi-Fi operators are limiting its usage (as the less it is used, the lower capacity – and therefore cheaper – the connection they need to the Internet). Some are blocking the use of Skype and other VoIP communications; some block Wi-Fi connections to a router on board, so you can just

VoIP

VoIP (making phone calls over the Internet) is an interesting phenomenon that has really picked up over the last year or so. If you have a dial-up, Wi-Fi or broadband connection, you can make phone calls for free or at low cost using your Internet connection (though obviously you still have the cost of the connection). Skype is the best known VoIP service provider, though there are many others to consider, such as Sipgate, Vonage and VoIPCheap. Most VoIP providers use a standard protocol (SIP) to make the calls over the Internet, and this enables you to use a standard phone with a network adaptor, a SIP phone connected directly to your Internet connection, or software on your PC with a headset. Skype uses its own proprietary protocol, and requires you to have your PC up and running, even if you connect a Skype compatible phone to your PC. Services offered include free calls to other people on the same VoIP network and cheap calls to 'normal' phone numbers. You can also have a phone number for incoming calls, voicemail, fax and so on, though these vary according to the supplier.

connect the Wi-Fi to a single computer (though that computer can then share the connection round the network). With BGAN, you just open up the unit and point the antenna at the satellite and, once locked on to the satellite, you make your phone calls.

KEEPING IN TOUCH

Coastal

At present, 'coastal communications' means one thing: mobile phones. Looking ahead, a long range version of Wi-Fi is being rolled out, called WiMAX or 802.16.

GSM

Mobile phones need no introduction – there are over 2 billion in use worldwide, and the chances of any readers of this book not having one are slim. In addition to the mobile phone we all know and carry, you can also get a fixed GSM unit, called an FCT (Fixed Cellular Terminal), such as the Ericsson F251M and Nokia 32. These just hold the SIM card and GSM technology, and you plug in a normal phone handset

Coverage map of Europe.

17

COMPUTERS ON BOARD

(or a DECT cordless phone), giving a fixed phone installation on your boat.

GSM stands for *Groupe Spécial Mobile*, the European group that set the standard to be used for mobile phones across Europe, instead of the multitude of operator-specific standards that were in use. Since that day in 1987, the mobile phone industry has become one of the fastest growing industries worldwide. At the latest count, 205 countries support the GSM standard, making up 75% of all mobile phones. There are other mobile phone standards in North America and Japan, though these countries also have GSM networks.

The GSM network operates by dividing the land up into a number of cells, and the maximum range of a cell is 22 miles. This is set by timing issues, not radio signal strength, so this limits the range at which you will be able to receive a signal. You can see coverage maps of all the GSM network operators at the GSM World web site (www.gsmworld.com) under the roaming section.

Theoretically this offers a range of 31 miles (50km) and 70Mbit/s, but as usual, hype does not match reality, and more realistic figures are 2Mbit/s, and a range of anywhere between 3 and 10 miles (5–16km). As with Wi-Fi, WiMAX will be used for VoIP-based phone calls, as well as data communications.

To get the maximum possible range, the only thing you can do is to fit an external antenna, with higher gain and greater sensitivity than the small stub antenna built into your phone. All FCT units support this, and some phones or car phone kits also have the ability to connect to an external antenna. The antenna will receive a weaker signal,

A fixed GSM phone module.

and when transmitting will ensure that more of the signal goes out horizontally rather than up into space – in this respect, the longer the antenna the better, but don't forget that sailing boats heel!

Because GSM signals are low power (just 1 or 2W), it is essential that the antenna is connected to the phone by high quality, low loss cable – RG58 for runs of a few metres, or RG213 for longer runs. GSM phones also operate in four frequency bands: 900 and 1800MHz in Europe, and 850 and 1900MHz in North America. It is important that your antenna is designed for the frequencies you will use.

When travelling abroad, your UK

KEEPING IN TOUCH

network will not be available, so you need to select a foreign network: this is called 'roaming'. Each network operator sets up roaming agreements with other operators abroad, so you cannot always use all of the available networks in the country you are visiting. Speak to your operator, or look at the roaming section in www.gsmworld.com, to view roaming agreements for the country you are visiting.

Mobile phone charges when abroad can be very high – even more expensive than a satellite phone. The EU is taking action to make these charges more reasonable, but in the short term we are stuck with them. The easiest way of getting round the charges is to get a local Pay As You Go SIM card for the country you are visiting (though obviously this isn't worthwhile for short visits), or you can now get special global roaming SIM cards from specialist providers. Also, using SMS (text) messages is much cheaper than phoning. Otherwise, speak to your operator before you go: sometimes you can pay a slight premium on your monthly bill to get significantly cheaper calls abroad. Also, call rates vary according to the network you use when abroad, so check which networks are cheapest for you to use.

Offshore

Most sailors find that when sailing around Europe, a mobile phone is fine, and they can live with short times out of mobile coverage. However, if you are looking to go further afield, you will no doubt consider a satellite phone.

As far as voice calls are concerned, there is little to differentiate the various satellite networks (though see the next chapter for data services, where there are significant differences). The primary factors for voice users are coverage, cost of equipment and calls. In terms of voice call quality, there are two main factors: satellite height, and the bandwidth

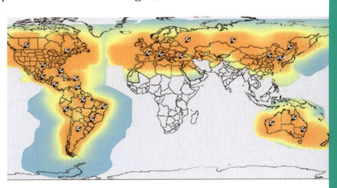

Globalstar: primary coverage in orange, single satellite/weaker coverage in yellow and sporadic coverage in blue.

allocated to each voice call. Satellite height affects timing, with the high orbit geostationary satellites such as Inmarsat, Thuraya and ACeS introducing a noticeable half second time delay between somebody talking and the person at the other end hearing them. Low Earth orbiting satellites from Iridium and Globalstar are close enough to the earth for there to be no noticeable time delay.

As regards voice quality, the higher bandwidth systems such as Inmarsat Fleet offer the same quality as GSM

COMPUTERS ON BOARD

mobile phones, whereas Iridium is noticeably poorer on voice quality (though still acceptable for normal conversations).

For worldwide coverage, the choice is between Iridium and Inmarsat. Iridium is generally the most popular, due to the

Inmarsat: global beam services within ellipses and spot beam services within darker blue, being rolled out to include the yellow.

smaller size and lower cost of its equipment, but if you are going to do a lot of data communications, or need web access rather than just e-mail, then Inmarsat Fleet is the better route. The Inmarsat mini-M system has largely been replaced by Iridium for

Thuraya: coverage everywhere within white line.

leisure users, but Inmarsat have just struck a deal with the far eastern ACeS satellite to roll its service out worldwide, and this will become Inmarsat's low cost, portable satellite communications system.

Of the non-global service providers, Globalstar covers all of Europe, the Middle East, North and South America, Australia and New Zealand, but does not give full coverage over the oceans. Thuraya covers Europe, the Middle East, India, and much of Africa, though experience shows that coverage in the more northerly parts of its map may be problematic. At present the ACeS system covers the Far East but, as mentioned above, after its takeover by Inmarsat it will be rolled out worldwide. Although restricted in coverage, these providers often offer

A Globalstar fixed installation.

KEEPING IN TOUCH

cheaper handsets and lower call costs than the global systems.

The table on the right compares typical costs for satellite hardware and call charges, all inclusive of VAT, but not including installation costs. There are generally a number of options for the hardware – I have worked on the basis of a fixed installation (or a handheld phone with a cradle), and an external antenna.

A handheld unit on its own is quite a lot

Satellite System	Equipment Cost (£)	Call cost (£/min)
ACeS	550	0.33–0.91
Globalstar	1,300	0.45–1.40
Inmarsat Fleet F33	5,000	0.60–1.25
Inmarsat Fleet F55	7,000	0.60–1.25
Inmarsat mini-M	2,500	0.80–0.90
Inmarsat BGAN	1,200	0.50–0.65
Iridium	2,100	0.55–1.15
Thuraya	600	0.50–0.70

less, but you will need to use it on deck, and will need additional items for connecting to your computer. Prices of hardware and charges can vary significantly with some systems – it pays to shop around.

MANAGING YOUR SYSTEM

> A simple and flexible approach is to add a small phone exchange

Whilst making the most of your communications, you may end up with a plethora of devices on board, and each one will potentially have its own handset. When someone calls the boat, you will have to find and answer the handset that is ringing. Conversely, when you want to call out, you will have to find the right device to make that call.

A simpler and more flexible approach for those with multiple comms devices is to add a small phone exchange (PBX). This is not to support a large number of users calling out through shared lines, as in a business environment, but rather to enable a few to easily use the outgoing connections they have. All outgoing phone connections, and all handsets, are attached to the PBX. The phones can be connected using either normal phone cabling, or they can share computer network cabling. Alternatively, wireless

COMPUTERS ON BOARD

phones can be used, connecting over either Wi-Fi or DECT. These are a good choice because they can be carried throughout the boat. With this system, once properly configured, any phone can be used to call out on any device. If that device is busy, it can either drop through to the next one in the list, or you can manually select an alternative device. For example, in harbour you can use Wi-Fi, then switch to mobile phone, and finally to satellite, as you require greater range and are prepared to pay a higher price. With incoming calls, regardless of which device the call comes in on, the PBX can ring one or all phones, and divert through to an answerphone if there is no answer.

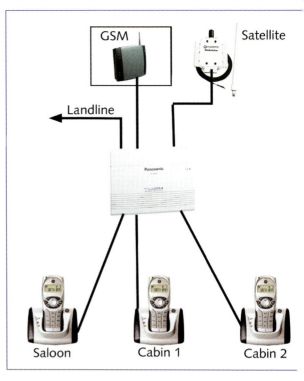

Installation diagram for a multiple PC network.

CALLS TO THE BOAT

When calling a mobile or satellite phone from a normal landline, the charges can be considerably higher than when calling out from the boat – calls to satellite phones from a BT line are billed at about £3.50/minute. Calling a mobile in the UK is fine, but when a user is abroad, the roaming charges are added to the bill.

It is almost always cheaper to have the phone call made out from the boat to the land destination. A useful trick here is to send a text message to the

An Iridium phone can be used anywhere in the world.

KEEPING IN TOUCH

mobile to say 'call me', or with an Iridium phone you can do this from the Iridium web site. Another option with Iridium is to have an Iridium phone on land as well as at sea, as Iridium to Iridium calls are charged at just 60p/minute. For a work environment, the Iridium phone can be wired into the office's PBX.

Another alternative, when the boat is in a suitable marina, is to have Skype or another VoIP service on board, and to sign up with a UK phone number. Now, anyone wanting to call the boat just needs to call the UK number, and the phone will ring on the boat, wherever it is in the world, as long as it is connected to the Internet (normally via Wi-Fi in the marina).

SUMMING UP

There are now many ways of keeping in touch, both when alongside and when at sea. For better or for worse, the days of being incommunicado from when you left the dock until you returned are long gone. With such a variety of choices, it pays to analyse your needs before committing to a system – and also to bear in mind the data capabilities of the system, as discussed in the next chapter.

USEFUL WEB SITES

VOICE OVER IP
Sipgate – www.sipgate.co.uk
Skype – www.skype.co.uk
VoIPCheap – www.voipcheap.co.uk
Vonage – www.vonage.co.uk

MOBILE PHONE ANTENNAE
AC Marine – www.acmarine.dk
Communication Aerials –
   www.communicationaerials.com
Procom – www.procom-dk.com

GSM ROAMING
0044 – www.0044.co.uk

EU site on roaming charges –
   europa.eu.int/information_society
   /activities/roaming/index_en.htm
Go-Sim – www.gosim.com
GSM World – www.gsmworld.com
Sim4Travel – www.sim4travel.com
TravelSIM – www.travelsim.org

SATELLITE PHONES
Globalstar – www.globalstar.com
Inmarsat – www.inmarsat.com
Iridium – www.iridium.com
Thuraya – www.thuraya.com
ACeS – www.acesinternational.com

COMPUTERS ON BOARD

CONNECTING TO THE INTERNET

You can connect to the Internet through any of the means discussed in the previous chapter, though you often have additional choices of speed and cost. Whereas with voice communications you just need to be able to speak to the person at the other end of the line, with the Internet, if your requirements are for live video conferencing the equipment you require will be very different from someone just needing to send a few e-mails.

WEB BROWSING OR E-MAIL?

When choosing between a mobile or satellite phone, your decision is generally based on the coverage for your cruising area, the hardware and call costs. With Internet access, there is a key additional parameter – will e-mail suffice, or do you want full web browsing capabilities? If you want the latter, you need a significantly faster connection than for just e-mail. Although you can just about

CONNECTING TO THE INTERNET

get away with the 9.6kbps of Globalstar and Thuraya, you really need a faster connection than this for anything more than occasional use.

How Fast Can I Go?

The table below gives the actual performance of each of the available systems. Although sufficient for comparative purposes, a number of factors mean that the performance you experience will never match the published figures, for the following reasons:

- ❏ The overheads of data communications mean that the data actually arriving at your machine will not match the maximum rate.
- ❏ Performance is affected by the delays of the Internet – the server at the other end may be sending out data at a slow rate if it is busy, and there may be delays at the remote server or at other points along the path, resulting in the connection feeling slower and less responsive.
- ❏ The mobile or satellite connection itself can have a delay, whether it is the time to travel up to a geostationary

Connection	Data rate (kbps)	Time for 1MB download (mins)	Data call (£/min)	Data call (£/MB)
Broadband	500–8,000	0.02–0.4 Likely to be limited by general Internet speed	N/a	N/a
Dial-up modem	Up to 50	4	0.02–0.04	0.08
Wi-Fi	2,000–15,000	Limited by general Internet speed	N/a	N/a
WiMAX	10,000	Limited by general Internet speed	N/a	N/a
GPRS	36	5.5	N/a	1–14
GSM	9.6	20.8	0.15–1.50	3.10–31.00

COMPUTERS ON BOARD

Connection	Data rate (kbps)	Time for 1MB download (mins)	Data call (£/min)	Data call (£/MB)
3GSM	300	0.7	N/a	1–14
HSDPA	1,000	0.2	?	?
Globalstar	9.6	20.8	0.45–1.40	9.40–29.20
Inmarsat BGAN	Standard 492	0.4	N/a	2.35–4.30
Inmarsat Fleet 33	Dial-up 9.6 MPDS	20.8	2.15	44.80
	64 download, 28 upload	3.1 7.1	N/a N/a	16 16
Inmarsat Fleet 55	ISDN 64 MPDS 64	3.1 3.1	4.70 N/a	14.70 16
Inmarsat Mini-M	2.4	83.3	0.80–0.90	66.6–75
Iridium	2.4	83.3	0.55–1.15	45.80–95.80
Thuraya	9.6	20.8	0.50–0.70	10.40–14.60

satellite and back, or the time delays in going through a GSM network.
☐ Some connections such as GPRS and 3G on a mobile phone, and Inmarsat's MPDS, are shared connections (just like Wi-Fi and broadband), so the more users there are at a given time, the slower the connection for each user.
To improve speed, you can use tools for data compression or for actually reducing the amount of data sent and received. Some service providers supply compression software, and they may quote performance figures that include an estimate of the compression benefits. To give a fair comparison, we have quoted the actual performance without compression, as all of the systems can have a compression tool added, even if not supplied by the service provider.

CONNECTING TO THE INTERNET

For some connections, such as Wi-Fi and broadband, download speeds are likely to be limited by the general speed of the Internet, and have not been given here. Mobile phone technology speeds are increasing – with a minority of phone models in the UK supporting 3GSM (3G), the next generation HSDPA is already rolled out in many countries (presumably only delayed here in the UK by the ridiculous amounts paid by the operators to the government for 3G licences), and the even faster HSPA is under development. Knowing the phone operators, we won't necessarily pay less for the data connections, but it will get much faster.

SETTING UP

Setting up your mobile connection is slightly different from setting up at home or in the office, as you cannot take it for granted that you have a fast, cheap connection. Here, some of the differences are discussed, and the next chapter takes you through a more hands-on configuration.

Because of the slow speed of the connection, you need to switch off automatic downloads, updates and log-ons from programs, only re-enabling them when you have a Wi-Fi connection or are back home. This includes things such as Windows Update, anti-virus updates, Windows Messenger and Skype. To test this out, connect to the Internet with no other programs running, and the figures for the amount of data sent and received should be pretty well stationary. If they are changing, either a program is talking to the Internet, or you have caught a virus.

When you are using your mobile phone abroad with GPRS or 3G, you will probably find that you

> **You cannot take it for granted that you have a fast, cheap connection**

cannot roam between networks as you can with voice calls and text messages. Check with your airtime provider before you go, to see who you should be using to connect. Once you have set up your phone with the required network, leave all the other settings alone – don't change them to those of the foreign airtime provider you are using.

There is more involved in setting things up on the water than with a home or office Internet connection, so if in doubt I strongly suggest you contact a company who has experience in setting up PCs with mobile phone or data connections (but beware – many marine electronics companies do not have the necessary computer skills in this area, and many mobile phone resellers know more about ring tones than data connections). A badly set up system will cause frustration and high comms bills, and all too often the equipment is blamed, whereas it is generally the case that the computer is not properly configured, or the user has not had enough training.

KEEPING THE COSTS DOWN

To help keep your costs down, many of the techniques discussed in the previous chapter apply – use the cheapest device you can, get a local SIM card for your mobile phone, etc. However, there are some additional tricks. Firstly, for short messages, the cheapest method by far is to send a text message from your mobile phone. Secondly, when selecting a local SIM card make sure it has GPRS capability – until recently GPRS was restricted to contract phones in most countries, though this is slowly changing.

In the table on pages 25–26, you will see the cost per minute, and the cost per megabyte. With newer packet-based technologies, such as GPRS, 3G and Fleet MPDS, you are billed for the actual volume of data sent and received, rather than the connection time. This is good news, as charges are not clocking up whilst a server sends you your e-mail or a web page, nor are you charged when reading a web page. On the other hand, for connections such as a dial-up modem, GSM, Fleet, ISDN, and the slower satellite phones, you are charged by the minute. To get a cost per megabyte for these connections, I have assumed the connection runs at about two thirds of the maximum speed.

PERFORMANCE ENHANCEMENT

There are a number of things that can be done to improve the efficiency of your connection, which can be broadly divided into: improving the efficiency of the underlying connection; reducing the amount of data sent and received; and compressing the data. These are not mutually exclusive – you can generally mix and match with different tools. The following tables give information about the main programs that are on the market, and the features they offer.

CONNECTING TO THE INTERNET

E-MAIL OPTIMISATION

Product	Reduce e-mail size	Mail compression	Converts HTML to text	Remove attachments	Header preview	E-mail client	Web mail	Retrieve other e-mail addresses	E-mail address
MailASail	Incoming	Bi-directional	Incoming	Incoming optional	No	Any	Yes	Yes	@mailasail.com
OnSpeed	No	Bi-directional	No	No	No	Any	No	No	Any
SmartCom	Outgoing	No	Outgoing optional	Outgoing optional	Yes	Any	Yes	No	Any or @smartcommail.com
UUPlus	Yes	Bi-directional	Yes	No	Yes	Any	No	Yes	@uuplus.com
zap	No	Yes	No	No	No	Outlook	No	No	@zap-email.com

COMPUTERS ON BOARD

WEB OPTIMISATION

Product	Compress web pages	Convert to plain text	Download web pages to PC	Notes
MailASail	No	Yes	No	Also offers an online blog
OnSpeed	Yes	No	No	
SmartCom	No	No	No	
UUPlus	No	No	Yes	
zap	No	No	No	

CONNECTION MANAGEMENT

Product	Connection manager	Network optimisation	Simultaneous send/ receive	Resume if line dropped	Auto adjust SMTP server	Notes
MailASail	No	No	Yes	No	No	Uses your existing ISP
OnSpeed	No	No	No	No	No	
SmartCom	Yes	Yes	Yes	Yes	Yes	Dialup number given, or use your existing ISP
UUPlus	Yes	No	Yes	No	No	
zap	Yes	No	No	No	No	Connects direct to Zap server

CONNECTING TO THE INTERNET

OnSpeed

Using technology from SlipStream in Canada, OnSpeed uses a server on the Internet and a small tool on your computer to compress both incoming and outgoing data, whether e-mail or web pages. The level of compression can vary enormously – zipped files and most image files will have little or no compression, whilst Word, Excel and plain text documents will compress to anywhere between 25% and 10% of their original size. OnSpeed has been marketed to dial-up customers wanting a faster connection, but it is of even greater benefit when used with a mobile or satellite phone.

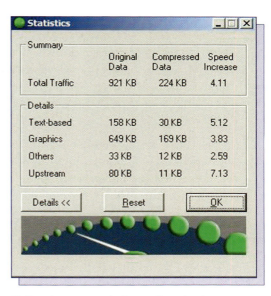

OnSpeed compresses both e-mails and web pages.

SlipStream's technology is also used in Iridium's Apollo 2 service (which is free but only works with Iridium), and some mobile phone operators use SlipStream or similar services on their networks, though this may be a chargeable option (for example Vodafone charge about £140 per year for their compression service).

SmartCom makes management of your Internet connections easy.

SmartCom

SmartCom is a software tool designed to make your mobile or satellite phone connection more efficient and easier to use. You create all of your dial-up, mobile phone and satellite connections within the SmartCom software, and then select the one you want to use from the menu. SmartCom then changes all the necessary settings behind the scenes, and connects you. It also tests for problems more extensively than Windows, and gives you understandable and helpful error messages.

31

To speed things up, SmartCom carries out a number of things 'under the covers':
- The low-level network settings are optimised for your chosen connection, as the various mobile and satellite phones all have very different optimum parameters from the dial-up connection Windows is designed for.
- Outgoing e-mails are reduced in size by removing all the unnecessary hidden information that Outlook places in the header. You can also ask SmartCom to convert outgoing e-mails to plain text, remove attachments, etc.
- E-mail is sent and received simultaneously (compared with Outlook, which sends and then receives) so you are online for a shorter time.
- If the Internet connection is dropped, SmartCom will pick up where it left off when you reconnect, whereas the standard behaviour is to start again from scratch, downloading things a second time.
- You have the option to set a size limit for incoming e-mails. Smaller e-mails are downloaded as normal, but for larger ones SmartCom downloads the header, and allows you to decide whether you want to delete the e-mail, leave it on the server for later, or download it.

SmartCom costs from £39 (with no annual fee) and if you wish, you can also have Internet access and your own e-mail address at smartcommail.com, complete with webmail access for when you are at a cyber café or another person's computer. SmartCom can be configured to work with other complementary tools, such as OnSpeed or MailASail.

SmartCom also manages your e-mail accounts.

MailASail

MailASail is designed primarily for high speed e-mail downloads, and for e-mail it complements the SmartCom system and adds the compression of OnSpeed (though at present it does not compress web pages). For incoming emails, it first carries out actions similar to what SmartCom does for outgoing e-mails, and then does a few more things, namely:
- All of the unnecessary header information is removed – this is generally larger than for outgoing e-mails.
- The text of the e-mail is converted to plain text.

CONNECTING TO THE INTERNET

- If there is an attachment in PDF or Word format, the text is extracted and added to the body of the e-mail.
- Attachments (except GRIB weather files) are removed and left on the server for you to pick up later via webmail.

Both incoming and outgoing e-mails are compressed, and sending and receiving is carried out simultaneously (as with SmartCom). With MailASail you have to use their e-mail address (eg fred@mailasail.com), though this can pick up e-mails from your existing account(s). You also have access to your e-mail via a web browser, and you can post text and pictures to a blog on the web, to give friends and family news on your cruise.

UUplus

UUPlus is an American package offering fast e-mail access. The e-mail handling is probably not as sophisticated and efficient as MailASail's, and the connection manager is not as powerful as SmartCom's, but it does offer both services in a single package. It also enables you to retrieve web pages you specify and send them to you compressed, but this is on a page by page basis rather than being done transparently for general web browsing.

zap

zap is marketed by AST Connections in the marine leisure sector (it is also used by commercial shipping). It operates slightly differently from the other programs: you dial in directly to zap's e-mail servers rather than via the Internet (except with connections such as GPRS), making it very fast and efficient. This is achieved by making the program an add-in to Microsoft Outlook – you cannot use Outlook Express or any other e-mail client. Compared with the competition it is relatively expensive, especially as you are charged for the volume of data regardless of whether or not it can be compressed (most image formats, for example, are already compressed). Also, because you dial in direct to their mail server, you cannot use the zap connection to access the web, and need a separate connection for this.

THE FUTURE

Many sailors and motorboaters expect that some day there will be broadband speed connections in the mid ocean using antennae a few inches across. With the combined laws of physics and economics, this will never be the case. There will always be a trade

COMPUTERS ON BOARD

off between data speed and costs (both capital and airtime), and each owner will make his decision dependant upon his needs. It is worth remembering, though, that it is always cheaper to send an e-mail than to give the same information over the phone or fax.

For the coastal boater, though, things are rapidly improving. Many marinas have Wi-Fi, and as WiMAX is rolled out, this can give coverage of about 10 miles/16km offshore. On the other front, mobile phone technology is also rapidly advancing, giving similar broadband speeds with better coverage, though at a higher price.

USEFUL WEB SITES

Product	Web site	Price
MailASail	www.mailasail.com	£140 per year
OnSpeed	www.onspeed.com	£24.99 per year
SmartCom	www.smartcomsoftware.com	From £39 one-off fee
UUplus	www.uuplus.com	£190 per year
zap	www.zap-email.com	£0.27/kbyte sent, max £70.65 per month

COMMS CONFIGURATION

Once you have your computer and comms hardware, you may think all is plain sailing, but many people come unstuck when configuring and commissioning their equipment. This chapter will take you through things step by step, highlighting many of the caveats and 'gotchas' that lurk for the unwary. Whether configuring a new system, or troubleshooting an existing one, go through things methodically from beginning to end and you should come out with everything working.

CONNECTING TO THE INTERNET

To connect to the Internet, you use an intermediary called an Internet Service Provider (ISP). The ISP will have a fast, high-capacity connection to the rest of the Internet, and will let you go through this to access the web. As options for connecting to the Internet have proliferated, so have the forms of the ISP.

COMPUTERS ON BOARD

With a normal dial-up Internet connection, as offered by your landline, GSM, and most satellite systems, you dial the ISP's phone number, your software sends the user name and password, the ISP allocates you a temporary IP address, and lo and behold, you are connected to the Internet. For this, you can use just about any of the many ISPs that are out there. You may want to stay clear of AOL and CompuServe, as their protocols are not standard and may not work with the compression services mentioned in the previous chapter. Services like AT&T and Pipex give you a local access number in many countries – it won't save you money

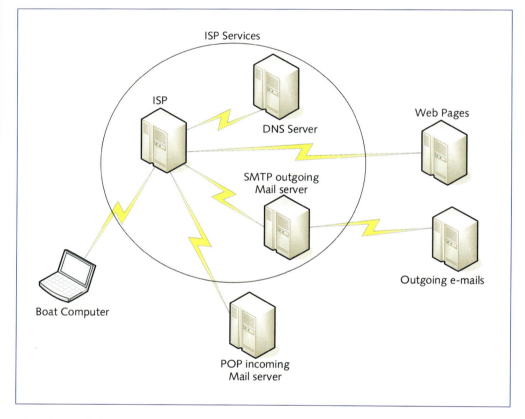

Internet connectivity.

with a satellite phone or when roaming with a mobile, but it will save you money if you use a land line (eg when in a hotel), or a local SIM card.

Some of the satellite system providers, such as Iridium, Thuraya and Inmarsat mini-M, give you a special access number (often a short code) to access the Internet, and they act as the ISP. Whilst you can also use your own ISP, using theirs generally gives a more reliable connection, and they can also help with troubleshooting.

COMMS CONFIGURATION

If you connect to the Internet via GPRS or 3G, or via Inmarsat's MPDS service on Fleet, rather than dialling out to an ISP, you are connecting directly to the airtime or service provider's network, and from there out to the Internet. For this reason, when setting up the Internet connection, the phone number can be left blank or as a random digit – the connection is set up with the extra configuration string added to the modem. Note that when using GPRS or 3G abroad, you do not need to change these settings; you only need to ensure that you select a network that has a roaming agreement with your home network provider.

Finally, when using Wi-Fi, you generally just need to select the network from the list of available networks (which may be other computers on other boats). This will then bring you to a home page, where you log in with your user name and password or, as a new subscriber, join up with your credit card details. If you cannot see the network on your PC, then there may be a weak signal where you are. Try taking the computer up on deck, or to other locations in the marina.

As options for connecting to the Internet have proliferated, so have the forms of ISP

If your laptop has Wi-Fi built in, it may not be the most sensitive piece of equipment. For the best reception, you need a Wi-Fi antenna up on deck, and this means using an external Wi-Fi adaptor, as the built-in ones cannot accommodate an external antenna.

Now you are connected, it is useful to check nothing is slowing you down unnecessarily. With your web browser and e-mail software *not* running, look at the counters for data sent and received. These should both be pretty well static, perhaps just occasionally going up by a few bytes at a time. If this isn't the case, check your Anti-Virus programme (see sections later in this chapter dealing with viruses, spam etc), as some other software on your computer is sending or receiving data in the background.

Domain Name Servers

Now you are connected to the Internet, the first thing to do is to open up your web browser and try to access a web page – Google is very reliable, and also downloads quickly due to its simple design. If it pops up, and does a search OK (so it isn't just showing a copy of the home page from the cache in your computer), then all is well and good. If not, you need to check your Domain Name Server (DNS) settings. The DNS is effectively a phone directory – you type in http://www.google.com, and the DNS changes this to Google's IP address of 66.249.93.99. Typing in http://66.249.93.99 works just as well, but is not as easy to memorise!

COMPUTERS ON BOARD

In general, when you connect to the Internet, your ISP will automatically tell your computer which DNS to use. However some ISPs (including many GPRS and 3G providers) use a static DNS, in which case you need to go and change the connection's network properties from getting the DNS address automatically, to setting it manually, and putting in the DNS address(es) of the service provider.

Web Browsing

You can now browse the web, but let's tweak things to make things faster (the following applies to Internet Explorer – other web browsers will have similar facilities). These are all made from the *Internet Options* dialog box.

First, set the home page to blank, so it doesn't start to download a page you probably don't want. You can also save time by saving regularly visited pages in your favourites.

Under the *Privacy* tab, enable the pop-up blocker, to stop new pages popping up on screen.

Under the *Advanced* tab, make variations from the default settings as follows:
- ❏ untick the boxes for automatically checking for Internet Explorer updates.
- ❏ untick the boxes for *Enable Install on Demand*.
- ❏ under *Multimedia*, untick the boxes for playing of animations, sounds and videos.

E-MAIL ACCOUNTS

The first thing to realise about e-mail is that your e-mail address is independent from how you access the Internet, even though most ISPs bundle the two together. So, once you have your preferred e-mail address, you can use it regardless of how you connect to the Internet.

You will generally get a standard SMTP/POP e-mail address: SMTP (Simple Mail Transport Protocol) is the means by which you send e-mails, and POP (Post Office Protocol) is how you receive e-mails. There are a couple of other options. Another mail protocol is IMAP (Internet Message Access Protocol). This alternative to POP is really designed for office applications, where you have a continuous connection to the

COMMS CONFIGURATION

server, as your e-mails stay on the server all the time, rather than being copied to your computer. In a mobile environment, this is slow and expensive, as whenever you want to read an e-mail, it is read from the server.

The other mail option that you may use at home is web mail, where you access your e-mail through Internet Explorer or another web browser. The great advantage of this is that you can access your mail through any computer with Internet access, but the drawback is that it works like an IMAP system but with the extra overhead of sending a full web page each time you go to a new e-mail. It is best used as a secondary method to your normal e-mail access – many ISPs and e-mail account providers offer this, or you can use a tool like www.mail2web.com if they don't.

Of the big ISPs, note that AOL uses IMAP, and can be configured to use Outlook for e-mail in preference to AOL's own user-friendly but slow interface. CompuServe offers POP3 if you use version 4 or earlier of their system; otherwise you are locked in to their proprietary protocol. Google's GMail offers POP3, but Hotmail now only offers it with their subscription accounts, not the basic free account.

Receiving E-mail

Setting up your PC to receive e-mail is generally very simple and straightforward. You just add a new account to Outlook, with the POP mail server, user name and password. As long as these are specified correctly, there should be no problems with receiving your e-mails.

> **Setting up your PC to receive email is very simple and straightforward**

One potential problem occurs when someone sends you a large e-mail: you don't know what it is until it is downloaded, and it will block any other e-mails from downloading in the meantime.

One solution is to preview e-mails larger than a certain size, so you have a choice of downloading the e-mail, deleting it, or leaving it on the server until later. Outlook has a basic ability to do this, but it tends to be slow and can get confused if many e-mails are left on the server. Third party tools such as SmartCom tend to be more robust. You can also use the MailASail service to strip off attachments, and convert e-mails to plain text, thereby circumventing the problem.

Another problem is that a mobile or satellite connection is more likely to drop the line than a normal dial-up line or broadband. If this happens, the behaviour of Outlook or any other standard e-mail software is to assume nothing was downloaded, and start again from scratch. Here, SmartCom fixes the problem,

COMPUTERS ON BOARD

by seeing which e-mails were downloaded successfully, and when reconnected telling the server to delete e-mails already downloaded to your PC, continuing where it left off before the interruption.

Sending E-Mail

It is when it comes to sending e-mail that many users stumble. The reason for this is simple: the SMTP that is used to send e-mail was developed in the heyday before spam was invented, and the ISPs who operate the mail servers today try to protect the servers from being used as spamming engines, sending out millions of spam e-mails. Because the protocol does not require the e-mail address of the sender (as included in the e-mail) to have any connection at all with the mail server, problems arise in determining who is a valid user of their mail server and who is not.

The SMTP was developed in the heyday before spam

The most common line of defence the ISPs take is to only allow you to send e-mail through their SMTP server if you have connected to the Internet through them. This prevents the spammers from having a computer on the Internet, sending e-mails through an ISP's SMTP server to make them look as if they have come from a genuine source. The drawback to the user is that every time they change ISP, say from a landline at home to Wi-Fi in the marina, to a mobile phone, they need to change their SMTP server settings in Outlook before they can send e-mail. This is a chore, though some programs such as SmartCom will do it for you.

Some ISPs may offer an alternative form of security: Authenticated SMTP. Here, they don't care whether or not you've connected to the Internet through them, but require you to use their SMTP server with a user name and password (often the same as your POP user name and password). This is particularly useful when connecting to the Internet via Wi-Fi, as most Wi-Fi operators do not offer an SMTP server, so you can use the Authenticated SMTP server from your dial-up connection, for example.

There are a number of things you can tweak to improve the performance of your email

Some ISPs will insist that you use their SMTP server, actively blocking you from using any third party server, authenticated or not. Orange, for example, do this with broadband, and some GPRS and satellite operators take a similar approach. Here you may have to register an e-mail address with them, not to use the e-mail address, but to allow you to access their SMTP service so you can send e-mails from your normal e-mail address.

COMMS CONFIGURATION

Optimising Outlook

There are a number of things you can tweak in Outlook or Outlook Express to improve the performance of your e-mail. All these changes are found under the *Tools/Options* menu.

First, go into *E-mail Options* under *Preferences*, and change the setting for replying to a message, so that it does not include the original text. The recipient wrote it, so why send it back to them?

Now, under *Mail Setup*, untick *Send immediately when connected*.

It is much more efficient to do this as one hit rather than for each e-mail, though you need to remember to click *Send/Receive*. Now click on the *Send/Receive* button, and untick *Schedule an automatic send/receive every xx minutes*. You can also set up e-mail groups so, for example, you can have a sailing group that excludes your work e-mail address.

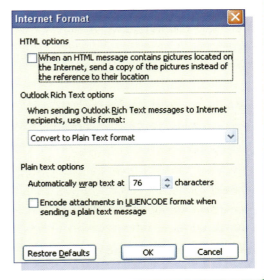

Now go to the *Mail Format* tab. Change the composing format to plain text, to make outgoing e-mails much smaller. Click on the *Internet Format* button, untick the first checkbox regarding images, and change the *Outlook Rich Text options* to *Convert to Plain Text Format*.

COMPUTERS ON BOARD

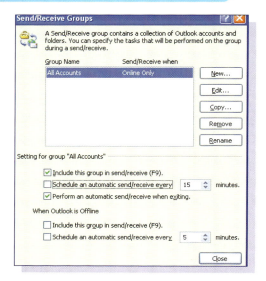 

Whilst here, some people like to add a signature asking senders not to e-mail large messages or attachments.

Finally, under the *Other* tab, disable the *Person Names* smart tag. Then, outside of

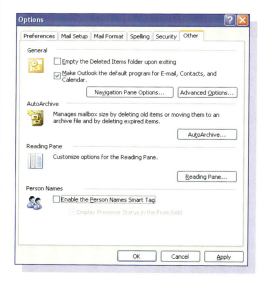 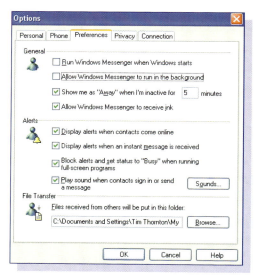

Outlook, go into *Windows Messenger's Options* dialog box. Under *Preferences*, untick *Run Windows Messenger* when Windows starts.

Unless you do both of these, Windows Messenger will be quietly running in the background, sending small amounts of data back and forth over the Internet even if you aren't using it.

COMMS CONFIGURATION

Configuring Smartcom

As an example of configuring one of the comms performance improvement tools, let's look at how to configure SmartCom (if you wish to try this, you can download a 30 day trial of the software from Smartcom Software's web site). Before doing this, I suggest that you get your basic Internet connection and e-mail up and running, otherwise you will not know if any problems are due to your basic settings being wrong, or the way you have set up SmartCom.

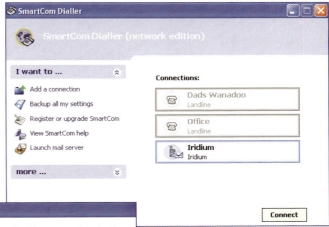

The next thing to do is to set up the dialler. If you have already set up your Internet connections, then click on *Add a Connection*, and import the existing connections.

When doing this, first select the type of connection (such as landline, GPRS, Iridium), then type in the user name and password, and also the outgoing (SMTP) mail server to use for this connection. You need to enter the SMTP server

COMPUTERS ON BOARD

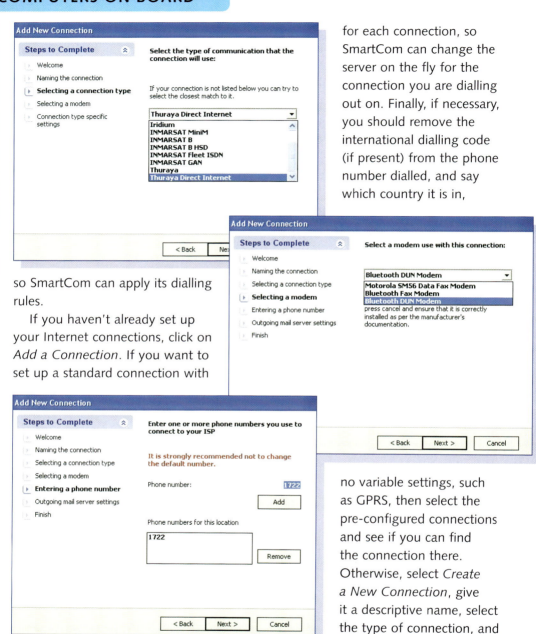

for each connection, so SmartCom can change the server on the fly for the connection you are dialling out on. Finally, if necessary, you should remove the international dialling code (if present) from the phone number dialled, and say which country it is in, so SmartCom can apply its dialling rules.

If you haven't already set up your Internet connections, click on *Add a Connection*. If you want to set up a standard connection with no variable settings, such as GPRS, then select the pre-configured connections and see if you can find the connection there. Otherwise, select *Create a New Connection*, give it a descriptive name, select the type of connection, and go through the wizard to select the modem, set the user name and password, the phone number(s) to dial, and the SMTP server.

You should now have a basic Internet connection for each connection method. Test these work correctly, before going on to set up your e-mail settings. If you go into

COMMS CONFIGURATION

General Settings, you can set the connection time-outs, optimise your TCP/IP settings to get the maximum data throughput for your connection, and also enable a log file for troubleshooting.

Now go on to the mail server. This sits between your e-mail client (such as Outlook or Outlook Express) and the Internet. The easiest way to set this up is to open up Outlook, and list your e-mail account details, then copy the settings into the SmartCom mail server.

In SmartCom, click on *Mailboxes*, and then *Add a new mailbox*. Now enter the mailbox user name, password, and e-mail address, and the incoming POP3 mail server. Once you have done this, go into Outlook, and set both the incoming and outgoing mail server to 127.0.0.1, which points Outlook towards SmartCom. At this stage, when you click on *Send/Receive* in Outlook,

COMPUTERS ON BOARD

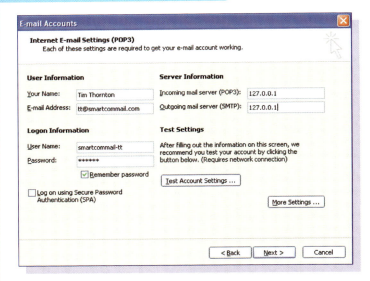

e-mails are sent to, and collected from, SmartCom, where they are stored until you go online. When you go online, SmartCom will immediately send and receive your e-mails to and from the Internet.

Finally, go into *Configuration*, where you can tweak your mail settings. The most important option is often the first one: *Configure the method of connection*. By default, this is set to use the SmartCom dialler, but if you want to use a network connection to the Internet, such as Wi-Fi, an office network, or some broadband connections, change this to: *Always try to send and receive messages*, and enter the SMTP mail server you wish to use. Now the SmartCom mail server will operate independently of the SmartCom dialler. *Configure the mail delivery process* allows you to control how often e-mails are sent and received when online. *Configure the cleaning policy* allows you to ensure outgoing e-mails are sent in the format you want, regardless of your settings in Outlook.

In Outlook, change the e-mail settings to send and receive e-mails automatically, so that they are immediately sent to the SmartCom mail server and stored there until you go online. Then, when you dial out with the SmartCom dialler, e-mails are sent and received as soon as you are connected and you also have your normal web browser Internet capabilities.

PROTECTING YOUR PC

Anti-Virus Software

A virus can be a disaster on board

Whilst getting a virus on a home or work PC can be a nuisance, if the virus sends out a lot of e-mails from your machine (which many do), it can be a disaster on board. As soon as your computer starts connecting to the Internet, the virus tries to send out huge amounts of e-mail or data, which either hogs all your bandwidth and stops

COMMS CONFIGURATION

you using the connection, or even prevents the logon process completing, so you cannot connect to the Internet.

A first line of defence should be your ISP – many, if not most, ISPs these days run anti-virus software on their servers, scanning incoming and outgoing e-mails. However, don't get too complacent: this will not protect you from viruses spread by means other than e-mail, whereas anti-virus software on your PC will.

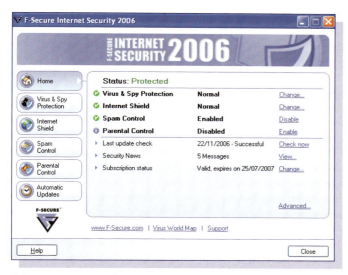

F-Secure anti-virus software.

There are many anti-virus products on the market. What you are looking for is something that won't slow your Internet connection down, and that also offers good technical support in the event you catch a virus. Some products are very user friendly, but slow as a result. A better bet are the packages aimed at small businesses from companies such as Sophos and F-Secure.

When configuring the anti-virus software, there are two recommended changes from the defaults. Firstly, do not scan outgoing e-mails. If your PC is clean, this isn't necessary, and it can slow down outgoing e-mails to such an extent that the SMTP server thinks you have disappeared, and drops the connection before your e-mails have gone out. Secondly, switch from an automatic download of updates to manual. This way, you can update your software when you have a fast, low-cost connection, such as Wi-Fi in the marina, or broadband at home.

Firewalls

You only used to really need a firewall if you were connected to the Internet for a long period of time, but this is no longer the case. However, the firewall included with Windows XP is a perfectly adequate tool.

To access the firewall settings, open up *Security Center in Control Panel*, then select *Firewall Settings*. Open up the security settings for *Windows Firewall*,

COMPUTERS ON BOARD

click on *Exceptions*, and untick all the boxes. This will lock down your computer, but may also prevent some perfectly valid programs from running.

Now, whenever a program tries to connect to the Internet, a message will come up advising you of this, and you can either block it or allow it through. The golden rules are: only allow programs that you recognise, and only allow the program if you know why it wants to connect to the Internet. If you don't recognise the program, or if you don't know why it wants to connect to the Internet, block it – you can always enable it later if you get this wrong. Doing this will stop programs sending usage data

SPAM

Everyone suffers from spam (or unsolicited e-mails). Some estimates say that as much as 80% of all e-mails are spam. The trick is to catch it at the server, rather than downloading it to your PC. Although Outlook has spam filtering tools, by the time it has been downloaded to your PC it has already added to your phone bill. Spam filtering needs to be done on the server, and an increasing number of ISPs have this as an option. The risk is that some bona fide messages will be trapped incorrectly, so you do need to monitor things and adjust the settings a bit.

Alternatively, if you are using a tool like SmartCom, you can just download the headers of files over, say, 2KB. The headers will download quickly, allowing you to delete the spam from the server before the full message is received. Although not as good as spam filtering at the server, this is better than nothing.

COMMS CONFIGURATION

to their server, downloading updates or other data-consuming activities, as well as helping to keep your computer free of viruses.

Spyware and Rogue Programs

An increasing number of software programs are written with the tacit assumption that you will be connected to a cheap, fast, broadband Internet connection. This connection is used to check for updates, to interact with servers on the Internet (eg to link with help files or databases of CD track names), or to give the developers feedback on your use of the program.

There are also spyware programs which will lurk on your computer unknown to you, and watch what you do. Their presence may be relatively innocuous, like tracking your use of the Internet to send information to ad agencies or launching pop-up ads, or it may be malicious, like trying to capture credit card details, or logon user names and passwords. It must be said that the majority of spyware programs are pretty innocuous, but a recent survey by AOL found that over 80% of home PCs had spyware of some sort installed.

We need to stop these programs, partly because of the effect on the performance and cost of your comms, and partly because of the potential theft of personal data. The first thing to do is to install some spyware detection and removal software, such as Lavasoft's Ad-Aware. Update it regularly, and run it once a week. Secondly, go into the *Options* settings of your programs, and make sure any options for connecting to the Internet are disabled. With this done, when you are connected to the Internet but are not doing anything, your counters for data input and output should be nearly static.

49

COMPUTERS ON BOARD

USEFUL WEB SITES

WI-FI
Wi-Fi Alliance – www.wi-fi.org
Square Mile –
   www.squaremileinternational.com

GSM
GSM World (for roaming and also mobile phone data technology) – www.gsmworld.com
Ross Barkman's GPRS Page – www.taniwha.org.uk/gprs.html

SATELLITE PHONES
Globalstar – www.globalstar.com
Inmarsat – www.inmarsat.com
Iridium – www.iridium.com
Thuraya – www.thuraya.com

SOFTWARE AND SERVICES
F-Secure – www.f-secure.com
Lavasoft (for AdAware) –
   www.lavasoft.de
MailASail – www.mailasail.com
OnSpeed – www.onspeed.com
SmartCom –
   www.smartcomsoftware.com
Sophos – www.sophos.com

WEATHER OR NOT TO SAIL?

Whatever your type of sailing, getting the weather right is indispensable to your safety and enjoyment. You may just want to know if rain is on the way, to decide whether to go out on the water or down to the pub. You may be planning a cross-channel trip, and want to make sure that the conditions will be both safe and (reasonably) comfortable. Or you may be a blue water sailor on a long passage, and knowing the weather forecast will help you prepare for bad weather, or remind you to check your fuel reserves for motoring. For all of these scenarios, up to date and accurate weather information is essential, though the information itself may be significantly different.

COMPUTERS ON BOARD

This chapter is primarily concerned with receiving weather information on the computer – there are plenty of alternative sources of information via radio broadcasts etc. This encompasses receiving official marine sources such as NAVTEX, SafetyNET and Weatherfax; the multitude of web sites; weather information services such as SmartMet; and weather in chart plotters such as seaPro, RayTech and MaxSea (including GRIB files). As well as looking at what is available, we will also look at hints and tips on how to get the best out of each service.

NAVTEX

Almost all yachtsmen are familiar with NAVTEX, and its transmission of the shipping forecast twice a day. In addition to seeing the NAVTEX messages on a dedicated

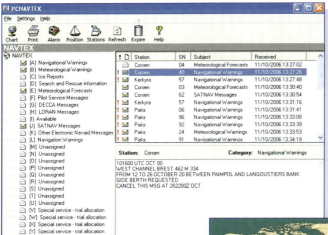

NAVTEX receiver and its LCD or printer, you can also do the same thing on your computer. Both NASA and Silva produce NAVTEX receiver engines, that have the antenna and receiver but no display. These can be interfaced to a serial port on the PC, and either display the messages with the basic software

PC NAVTEX brings NAVTEX messages onto your PC.

provided, or use PC Navtex, which is a more powerful program. You can also interface your computer to standard NAVTEX receivers with a display or print-out from Furuno and McMurdo (previously ICS), to help provide a totally computerised system.

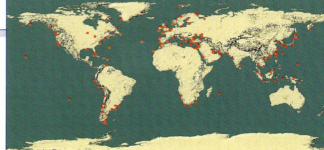

NAVTEX stations around the world.

Most NAVTEX transmitting stations are limited to a range of about 250 miles (402km). The frequency used does not propagate well over the land, so you will

WEATHER OR NOT TO SAIL?

often find poor reception in estuaries and marinas – the NAVTEX specification says it is designed for use to seaward of the fairway buoy, so operation in harbour should be seen as a bonus.

INMARSAT C SAFETYNET

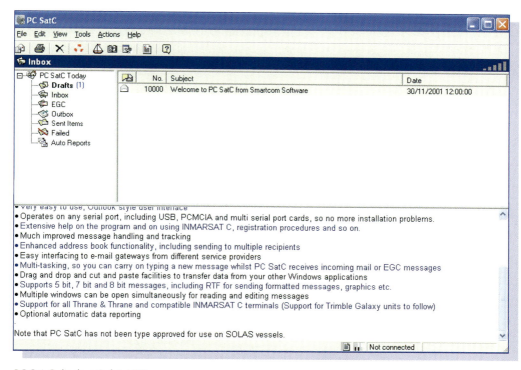

PC Sat C displays SafetyNET messages.

If you are sailing offshore, you will quickly get outside the 250 mile/402km range of most NAVTEX stations. However with Inmarsat C you can pick up the offshore version of NAVTEX messages – SafetyNET. These messages are identical to NAVTEX, but generally cover a larger area with a lower level of detail, and are more geared towards offshore information. You will receive these with your Inmarsat C software: PC Sat C or easyMail for Thrane & Thrane units, or Nebula for Trimble and Marconi units. Full details of both NAVTEX and SafetyNET transmissions can be found in the Admiralty List of Radio Signals. An excellent web site on NAVTEX and many other things weather-related is Frank Singleton's: www.franksingleton.clara.net

COMPUTERS ON BOARD

WEATHERFAX

Weatherfax is the third 'traditional' method of receiving weather data, though it is reducing in popularity, partly because the countries that operate Weatherfax stations want to close them down to save money, and partly because users are increasingly in favour of the ease of use and convenience of NAVTEX and Internet-based services. However, as with NAVTEX and SafetyNET, the information is free to receive once you have the necessary radio and software. You need an SSB radio receiver (or a full transceiver works just as well) and antenna, plus Weatherfax software. There is a wide range of Weatherfax software available, including commercial products from CombiTech, Xaxero and Bonito, and shareware packages from ham radio enthusiasts – see the list of web sites below for suppliers. Weatherfax consists of weather maps broadcast over SSB radio, and are great for a broad-brush weather forecast over a large area, but are not as detailed as some other sources. Weatherfax software will generally also receive NAVTEX messages, RTTY text weather data, and (with some software) SYNOP current weather reports.

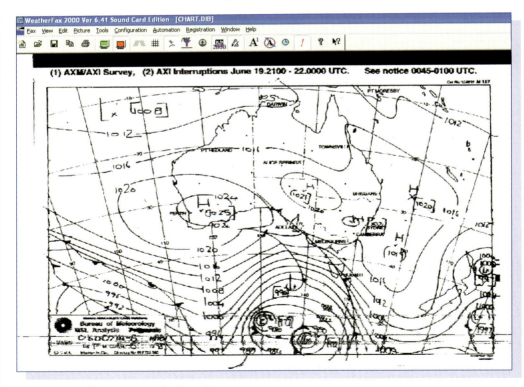

Xaxero Weatherfax 2000 Weatherfax software.

WEATHER OR NOT TO SAIL?

To use Weatherfax, you select the best frequency from those used by the transmitter, and tune in the radio (either manually or through the computer, depending on the software and the radio you use). The software then receives the fax, which takes about 10 minutes for each image to come through. As always with SSB radio, there is a bit of fiddling around in selecting the right frequency and tuning in the radio, and once the radio and computer are interfaced you should allow yourself half a day to get to grips with them. After this, use is easier, but it always requires a bit of adjustment to get the best out of the system. You will find details of broadcast schedules and frequencies in the Admiralty List of Radio Signals. Another very useful source of information on Weatherfax is the web site www.hffax.de

INTERNET SOURCES

The future for weather information is definitely moving towards the Internet. Weatherfax is steadily being shut down, and broadcast services cannot give the same level of on-demand, high resolution forecasts that Internet based services can provide.

Web Browsing

Now we can turn to the use of the Internet, and the choice here is between web browsing, and using software that downloads the data you want from the Internet, and then lets you browse it off-line.

On the web browsing side, there is a plethora of sources – Google gives over 2 million pages if you search for

> **You often get data free of charge from the US, whereas through the Met office you would have to pay for it**

weather forecast – and the problem is deciding what to look at. A good starting point is Westwind at www.westwind.ch, which is basically a database for weather forecasts around Europe.

For high resolution, detailed forecasts, WindGuru and Theyr are excellent.

Both companies run their own high resolution weather forecast model, and make the data available through their web sites for a small subscription. Other sites giving current weather reports include Chimet, and the NOAA and NDBC sites (you will find that, due to differences in government policies, you can often get data free of charge from sites in the US, whereas through the Met Office site you would have to pay for it). Finally, another useful site that brings together both forecast and current weather reports is the MIDAS Weather one – but there is a lot of data for Europe.

55

COMPUTERS ON BOARD

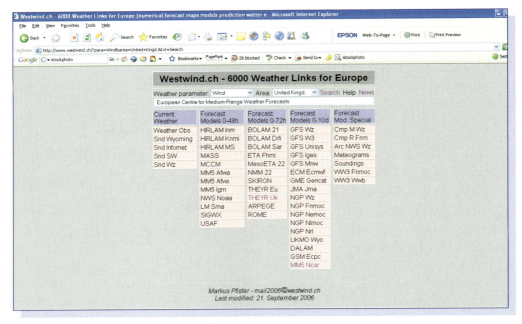

Westwind is an invaluable source for weather maps in Europe.

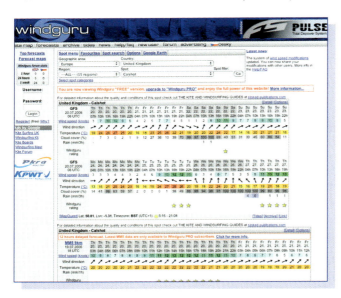

WindGuru gives detailed weather forecasts.

When looking at weather forecasts on the web, you should be aware of a few things. First, several sites may use the output from the same weather forecast models, but draw the maps in a different style – you may often think that you are comparing two forecasts, but they could actually be showing the same data. Here the Westwind site is very useful, as it shows which site uses which weather forecast model.

Also, be aware of the limitations of the model. Broadly speaking, there are two types of forecast model in use: 'synoptic models' that generate world forecasts, and 'mesoscale' models such as NAM (previously called Eta) and MM5 that produce more localised forecasts. Not only is the

WEATHER OR NOT TO SAIL?

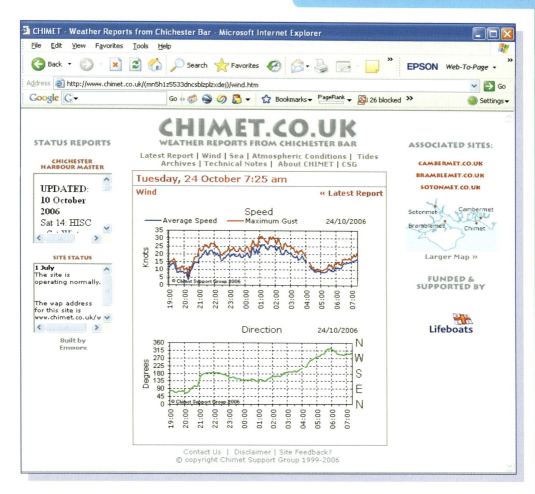

Chimet is one of a series of weather reporting sites along the English Channel.

resolution of the mesoscale models higher, but the physics of the model is also better, so the forecasts are generally more reliable. They take better account of the shape of the land, and have a better modelling of thermal

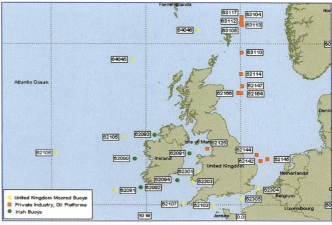

Weather buoy stations around the British Isles.

57

COMPUTERS ON BOARD

effects, such as land and sea breezes, thermal winds such as the Mistral, and thunderstorms. Synoptic models will have a resolution of 1–0.5 degrees, and 3 hour time steps, whilst mesoscale models may have a resolution of 0.2 degrees or less, and 1 hour time steps.

On the subject of resolution, a forecast model will typically only model land and sea areas that are about 4 times the size of the grid spacing, so the commonly used GFS model will not show the Isle of Wight, or the eastern half of the English Channel, and the high resolution Theyr model will only take into account features larger than 0.8 degrees in size. Unfortunately, some programs interpolate the GRIB data, implying that the forecast is more accurate than it really is. You need to be aware if this is happening in your software, and ensure that you do not make any wrong assumptions about the weather as a result.

Forecasts are not the only useful sources of weather information on the web. At least as useful for the immediate term are current weather reports, and these may come from a number of sources. On the surface, there are land-based weather stations, weather buoys, and ships reporting current weather conditions. From satellites, we can now have satellite images every 15 minutes showing both visible and infra-red images, fog and cloud maps, and the QuickSCAT sensor gives us wind speed and direction over the sea.

The BBC web site: a mine of useful information.

WEATHER SOFTWARE

The big drawback with looking at weather on the web is that the page downloads are fairly large, and therefore slow and expensive. This brings us on to weather software, where the weather data is downloaded to the PC in a compact format, and you can then view it offline. Although there is a fee for this software, it is often less than what you spend on your comms bill if you use a mobile or satellite phone, so the software can more than pay for itself.

There are some dedicated weather packages available, and some chart plotters offer a weather overlay facility. For forecast data, the GRIB file format is often used. This is a fairly compact standard file format for exchanging weather forecast data,

WEATHER OR NOT TO SAIL?

and many programs will either download, read or export GRIB files. Note that GRIB is a broad standard, and not all programs will read all GRIB files. GRIB files may be downloaded free of charge from sites such as MaxSea's navcentre.com or Raymarine, or you can request the data you want via e-mail, using services such as Saildocs or Global Marine Net. However, these are the low resolution GFS and WW3 files, and they may not be high enough resolution for weekend boating.

Of the dedicated weather packages, Nowcasting gives high resolution wind and wave data, and is great for use on passage on short trips, but the inability to see pressure or other data, and its user interface, makes it less useful as a planning tool. At the other end of the spectrum, BonVoyage and Moving Weather both use just the low resolution GFS and WW3 data, so give a good overall perspective on the weather, but lack detail for day sailing (Moving Weather interpolates the data to give the appearance of higher resolution). OCENS has a wealth of data, but much of this is for North America, and European coverage is less good, whereas both Navimail and SmartMet offer good detailed coverage of Europe. Navimail provides forecasts as GRIB files, text files, reports, and a satellite image, and is at its best in French waters. SmartMet covers the world, and as well as high and low resolution forecasts it also offers a comprehensive range of satellite images and current weather reports.

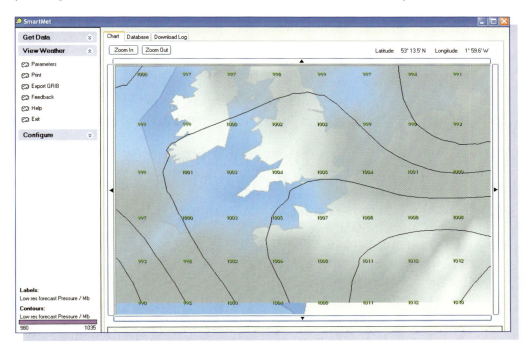

SmartMet gives you a wide range of weather information on your PC.

COMPUTERS ON BOARD

WEATHER ON YOUR MOBILE

If you want the easiest way of checking the weather, without having to wait for a scheduled broadcast or to boot up your PC, then use your mobile phone. A basic text forecast is available through many of the mobile phone operators and the European Met Offices. Alternatively, a tool like PocketMet will give you access to Europe-wide high resolution weather forecasts and the latest satellite imagery, in a clearly represented, graphical format.

PocketMet brings weather forecasts to your mobile phone.

A number of chart plotters will also display weather data over the chart, and some of these (such as seaPro, Deckman and MaxSea), will also use the weather data for weather routing. Although the visualisation of the weather data may not be as good or as comprehensive as in the dedicated weather programs, it can be useful to see the weather displayed over your route. Chart plotters will be dealt with in more detail in the next chapter.

CHOICES

As a user, you need to decide how much to use the data sent out free of charge in forms such as NAVTEX and Weatherfax, with its limited range of information, and scheduled transmission times, against how much to use Internet-based sources with their richer content and easier accessibility, but also with associated costs. Most weekend boaters will use both: primarily Internet-based services prior to departure, and a combination of the two en route. What you can be sure of, though, is that whatever weather information you may need, it is out there somewhere!

WEATHER OR NOT TO SAIL?

USEFUL WEB SITES

BBC weather web site – www.bbc.co.uk/weather
Chichester Bar current weather reports – www.chimet.co.uk
Frank Singleton's web site, full of useful weather info –
   www.franksingleton.clara.net
Global Marine GRIB files – www.globalmarinenet.net
Weatherfax information web site – www.hffax.de
UK Met Office web site – www.metoffice.gov.uk
Midas Weather current reports and forecasts – www.midasweather.com
Weather buoy data – www.ndbc.noaa.gov
Saildocs GRIB service – www.saildocs.com
Theyr weather forecast web site – www.theyr.net or www.theyr.tv
European weather forecasts and reports – www.webmet.com
Westwind weather forecast site – www.westwind.ch
Wind guru weather forecast web site – www.windguru.com
Current weather reports – www.xcweather.com

SUPPLIERS

Bon Voyage – www.appliedweather.com
Bonito – www.bonito.net
CombiTech MScan Weatherfax software – www.mscan.com
Midas Weather for SmartMet, PocketMet and WebMet –
   www.midasweather.com
Moving Weather – www.movingweather.com
Navimail GRIB service –
   www.meteofrance.com/FR/services/navimail/index_en.jsp
Nowcasting – www.nowcasting.ie
OCENS – www.ocens.com
PocketMet mobile phone – www.pocketmet.co.uk
SmartCom software for PC Sat C and PC NAVTEX –
   www.smartcomsoftware.com
SmartMet – www.smartmet.co.uk
Thrane & Thrane Inmarsat C systems – www.tt.dk
Xaxero Weatherfax and weather satellite software – www.xaxero.com

COMPUTERS ON BOARD

NAVIGATION

Mention using a PC for navigation, and people immediately think of chart plotters. It used to be the case that PC-based plotters offered significantly better facilities than dedicated electronic plotters, but the differences are no longer so clear cut.

PLOTTERS

PC-based plotters broadly fall into two categories. At the entry level, products from the likes of the UKHO, Euronav, Imray and Maptech include all the basic chart plotting facilities at a budget price (often as little as £50, including a basic folio of charts), or you can download DigiBOAT's SOB software for free (excluding charts). These carry out all of the functionality of a basic stand-alone electronic plotter, at a very affordable price, even if you include the cost of buying a laptop.

PC-based Plotters

The higher-end PC plotters add a variety of functions – depending on the equipment you have on board and the type of sailing you do, these may or may not prove useful. Interfacing capabilities

NAVIGATION

are greatly extended to include all of your instruments (not just GPS), AIS receivers, radar ARPA targets and full radar overlays. Both tide heights and tidal streams may be available, as well as course to steer and predicted ground track. Weather forecasts may be drawn over the charts (generally using GRIB files, as described in the previous chapter), and this may be extended to offer full weather routing as well. Manufacturers in this group include Euronav, Furuno (for MaxSea interfacing to Furuno NavNet radar and other instruments), MaxSea and Nobeltec. There are also other specialist packages for the yacht racing market, such as B&G's Deckman. The pricing of these higher-end products starts at about £400, depending on which optional modules you want to include. This works out considerably cheaper than an equivalent electronic plotter, even if you have to include the cost of buying the computer.

Electronic Plotters

Electronic plotters used to offer less functionality and less legibility than most PC-based plotters, but this is slowly changing. Displays are slowly getting larger and higher in resolution, though they still lag behind even entry level laptops. Also, the richer chart content from C-Map (NT/MAX and MAX Pro) and Navionics Platinum charts means that plotters now include almanac information, tidal heights and streams, aerial photos and 3D views, in the same way that many of the higher-end, PC-based plotters do. Finally, manufacturers generally offer radar integration at a lower price than the PC-based plotters, though you do have to use the same manufacturer for radar and chart plotter.

The first consideration is where you want to use the plotter

Which Route to Go?

The first consideration is: where do you want to use the plotter? You pay a considerable premium for the waterproof enclosure of an electronic plotter, and if there is so much water down below that you need a waterproof plotter, you probably have other things to worry about! On the other hand, if you want to navigate in the cockpit, although companies such as KS Bootronik and Raymarine make good quality waterproof, sunlight-readable PC screens, this reduces the price differential. A popular configuration on many yachts is to have a waterproof electronic plotter in the cockpit, and a PC down below at the chart table.

COMPUTERS ON BOARD

There are also some key differences in functionality and chart support. Electronic plotters do not support features such as tidal stream/course to steer calculations, weather overlays and routing, sailboat performance features, or the display of raster charts. If you want any of these, then you need to go the PC route – this may become more significant as we see increasing online services. Another factor is the user interface. The richer user interface, faster performance and ease of use of the mouse and keyboard are all benefits for PC users, and some packages such as Nobeltec's Admiral offer an alternative interface more suited to touch screens or a waterproof pointing device on a cockpit screen. Each software package has its own style of user interface, and you may want to look at a number to see which you prefer.

The PC-based chart plotter market has matured over the last few years. The technical novelty has gone, and PC-based chart plotting is seen as commonplace. Also, we no longer have the hugely overcrowded market there used to be, with players such as Transas and Chartworks having pulled out or closed down. Many of the remaining products are owned by major players: Nobeltec by Jeppesen, who are owned by Boeing; RayTech by Raymarine; and Furuno now hold a stake in MaxSea. As each player gets a bigger market share, there should be more money to produce higher

Northstar offer a detailed PC-based navigation system using Nobeltec software.

NAVIGATION

quality, better tested software, which has not always been the case in the past with both large and small players.

Some people have qualms about the reliability of using their PC for navigation. If the PC is treated like a dedicated instrument, so you just install the software you need, and just run the programs you need, then you will find it reliable. If, on the other hand, you are always trying out new programs, installing downloads from the web, plugging in new hardware, tweaking Windows settings and so on, then there will inevitably come a time when there is a problem. Computer reliability is generally something that is in the user's hands! Also, safeguards should be no different from using an electronic plotter – always carry sufficient paper charts, and always keep a written log of your position.

Assuming you are going the PC route, let's now look at some of the features you may expect to find on your chart plotter.

Charts and Other Information Sources

For sailing round Britain, nearly all of the chart formats will give you all the detail you need. It is really just a matter of looking at the price, how up to date the charts are, and the style of presentation. If you sail further afield, then it is worth looking

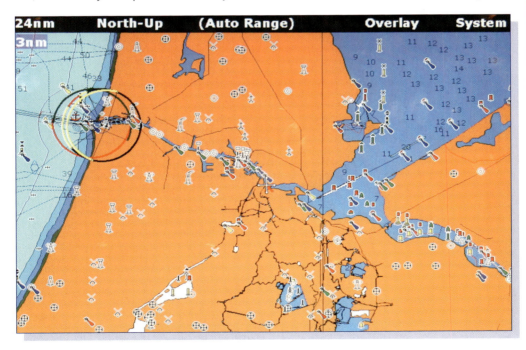

Chart plotter.

COMPUTERS ON BOARD

more closely at the coverage of the different chart providers, as this can vary considerably.

Many chart plotters offer a choice of formats, as well as adding aerial or satellite photos that can be overlaid on top of the charts, and 3D views of land and sea. Whilst none of this is strictly necessary, the photos can be a great help when orienting yourself in a new location, and the 3D views will give you a much better feel for the shape of the sea bed. As mentioned previously, the problem the chart producers have is that, whilst a lot of this data is available at minimal cost in the USA, because of different government policies the same data can be very expensive to licence in Europe.

There has long been a split between proponents of vector and raster charts. Neither is better; each has their own pros and cons. Raster charts are visually more pleasing to

ROUTES, WAYPOINTS AND AUTOPILOTS

All chart plotters have the ability to create routes and waypoints and, once you have created a route, most will also send NMEA data to the autopilot, to have it follow your route.

A useful extra facility is the ability to exchange routes and waypoints with your GPS or electronic chart plotter. This means that you can use one device as a backup for the other. It also enables you to use the powerful facilities of your PC for passage planning, whether at home or on board, and then upload the route and waypoints to your electronics, so you don't need the power drain of your PC running all the time. Unfortunately, there are a few possible snags with this. There are a number of NMEA sentences for routes and waypoints, and not all systems (whether PC or electronic) support all sentences. Even if they do, there is no standard format for waypoint and route names, so you generally need to ensure that waypoint names in the PC match any limitations that may occur in your plotter. You may also find that if a route or waypoint name is already in use in the plotter, it will not be overwritten when you send new data down from your PC. And, finally, some plotters are sensitive to timing, and if the PC sends the data down too fast, the plotter may not be able to keep up. If it all works, it's great. If not, the chances are each manufacturer will say that their product complies with the NMEA specification, and you'll have to accept that you won't get anywhere.

NAVIGATION

use and easier to read, as long as there are enough charts of different scales to cover the different zoom levels. Without enough charts of different scales, text and symbols can be too large or too small as the chart is zoomed in and out. Vector charts do not look as good graphically, but can be layered and queried, to add some intelligence to the system. Also, the file sizes are smaller, which is why they are used exclusively on electronic chart plotters.

> Looking ahead, I can envisage new technology developing in the form of hybrid charts

Looking ahead, I can envisage new technology developing in the form of hybrid charts, where layered raster charts are used for presentation, with an underlying database allowing items to be queried, and intelligent tasks such as checking your planned route for hazards.

In addition to the chart data itself, we are seeing the beginnings of a move to making the chart plotter a centre for all of your information needs. For example, C-Map have long included basic information on facilities (though with this stored on the chart cartridges, it quickly becomes out of date), and some plotters allow for integration of other information sources such as weather and NAVTEX messages.

An example of what is to come is a project called ALIS (At Sea Location Based Information Systems, sponsored by Galileo) to see how far information systems can be developed. Using an Internet connection, you can receive weather forecasts, navigation warnings, chart corrections, marina berth availability notifications, sailing instructions and local shore-based facility information. This is becoming increasingly feasible, with Wi-Fi in the marinas, the long-range WiMAX being rolled out, and the cost per megabyte of mobile and satellite phone communications dropping all the time. Interestingly enough, the next generation of GMDSS services are also likely to be based on standard Internet connections as well. You can find more information on the ALIS project on their web site, listed in the chart section of web links below.

Tides

As a starting point, most of the higher-end chart plotters will display tidal streams on the chart, and also give a curve of tide heights. However, most will offer additional features.

For tidal planning, most will calculate the course to steer corrected for the tide. Euronav's seaPro takes this further on two counts: it will give the predicted track over the ground, and also look at different departure times to see what effect this has on your passage time. No matter how much you like sailing, most people would agree that there is no fun banging your head against a foul tide.

COMPUTERS ON BOARD

Some programs, such as Nobeltec and MaxSea, will take the input from your GPS, log and compass, and calculate the actual tidal stream under the boat. It is interesting how often this is quite different from the tidal diamonds on the chart!

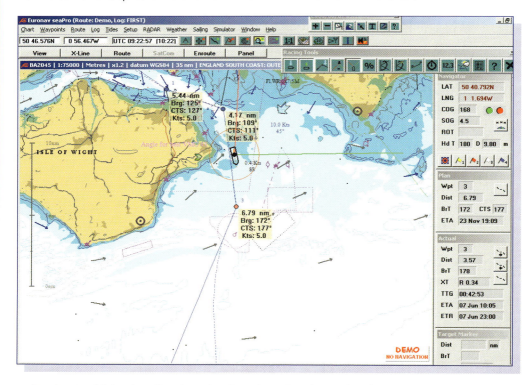

seaPro showing tidal vectors, the planned route and a projected ground track.

SAILBOAT PERFORMANCE

Although many people see performance programs as the preserve of the yacht racing fraternity, they are just as useful for the cruising yachtsman, and should not be dismissed out of hand. The difference is that the racing yachtsman will spend a lot more time with these tools, trying to squeeze out that last bit of boat speed or tactical advantage, whereas the cruiser will generally want a more relaxed approach to their time on the water. Sailing performance tools are generally an optional add-on to navigation packages such as seaPro or Nobeltec, though there are dedicated race packages such as B&G's Deckman.

NAVIGATION

Performance Monitoring

A basic feature of all of these tools is monitoring and graphing what is happening to factors like the wind and your boat speed. Showing a time plot of true wind speed and direction will help you see if the wind is changing or shifting.

Another useful pair of plots are your boat speed and compass heading. If speed is dropping off, you can tweak the sails to bring it back up again. If the helmsman is getting tired, you can normally spot this, with the graphs becoming more erratic. They may say they are fine, but big brother is watching them!

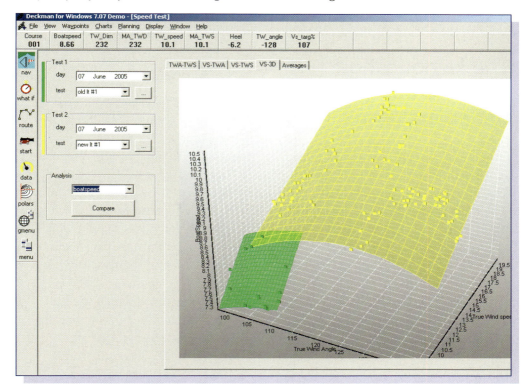

Deckman performance monitoring.

If you sail in tidal waters, you may also be interested in the geographical wind, especially in light airs. This takes out the effect of the tide from the true wind, so you can see if the actual wind over the ground is changing, and anticipate any changes in the true wind as the tide changes. To visualise this, imagine running dead downwind in a very light 3 knot wind, steering due south, at slack water. At this point the true and geographical winds are the same. When the tide turns, let's say you have 3 knots of east-going tide. Although the geographical wind has not changed, the true wind

COMPUTERS ON BOARD

will now be the combined effect of the geographical wind, and the tide pushing you through the air, so your instruments will measure 4.2 knots at 45 degrees off the port quarter. Six hours later, with the tide in the opposite direction, the true wind will be 45 degrees off the starboard quarter. Thus we have a increase in wind speed of 42% from the geographical wind, and all in all a 90 degree wind shift.

For those in tidal waters, many sailing performance packages will also calculate the tide under the boat, by comparing the GPS ground track against the course and speed through the water measured by your log and compass. Although this reading is damped down and does not display changes immediately, a plot of this will tell you when the tide is turning, and when you have got far enough inshore to avoid the worst of the tide, or to pick up a favourable back eddy.

The key question is where do I get the polars from?

Polars

Polars are simply a table showing your boat's speed over a range of wind speeds and angles. They serve two purposes: to give you a measure of how well you are sailing, and to allow for navigation planning taking into account your boat's performance in different conditions. Top notch race boats will use polars for other things like sail selection, but that is really beyond the scope of most sailors.

For monitoring performance, you can graph your actual performance against your target speed from the polars. Also, when beating and running, you can get your optimal true wind angle for maximum VMG. Depending on the conditions, you won't always be able to hit your targets, but your performance should always be a consistent percentage of the polars.

On the navigation front, when planning a route, the software should use the polars to look up the target speed for each leg of the course. Furthermore, the software can use the polars to pick up the best tacking and gybing angles for the current wind speed, and draw the tacking and gybing laylines on the chart. This will immediately tell you whether you can clear that headland, and also indicate when to tack or gybe so you don't overstand your next waypoint. Polars are also fundamental to weather routing, discussed below.

The key question is: where do I get the polars from? The designer will often provide theoretical polars for the boat, which can form a reasonable starting point, but they are seldom accurate enough for use on board. The only accurate method is to monitor the boat's performance when sailing well, and adjust the polars accordingly. To help with this, some programs like seaPro have tools to automatically update the polars. This should be seen as an ongoing process, as it takes many sailing hours to cover the whole gamut of wind speeds and angles.

NAVIGATION

WEATHER AND WEATHER ROUTING

Many chart plotting packages can overlay the chart with weather forecast data, generally in the form of GRIB files. You can decide which parameters to display, such as wind or pressure, and step through in time to see what the weather conditions will be en route. Some plotters, such as MaxSea, Raymarine and Nobeltec, include tools to download GRIB files, or you can use any of the sources given in the previous chapter.

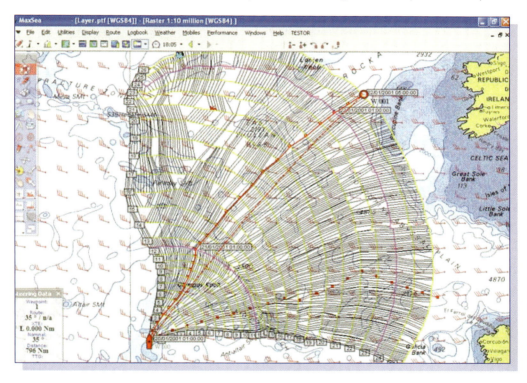

MaxSea weather routing calculates the fastest route, in red.

Weather routing takes the route calculation process one step further, not just sailing down the rhumb line but allowing the boat to take any course required to make the best passage time. Given a course, a date and time of departure, a weather forecast, tidal streams and your polars, the computer steps forward in time, looking where you can get to hour by hour until you arrive at your destination (or get to the end of the weather forecast). The programme then steps backwards in time, to see the route taken to get to your destination.

This is potentially a very useful tool, but there are a number of caveats. First, it

COMPUTERS ON BOARD

relies on reasonably accurate polars – if these are inaccurate, the results are not too meaningful. Secondly, the weather forecast needs to be correct. Finally, you need to look at the resolution of the forecast, which needs to be high enough to match the scale of your sailing. For example, a trip across the Solent cannot be planned with a global forecast, with data points every one degree and three hours: you really need a very high resolution forecast for this.

RADAR AND ARPA

Having the radar overlaid on the chart has a number of advantages

To fully integrate all your navigation capabilities, you may well want to add radar to your chart plotter. This can either be in the form of a full radar overlay on the chart, or just plotting the ARPA radar targets on your chart.

Plotting the ARPA targets is the easier option, as the target information is supported by standard NMEA sentences. Assuming your radar outputs these, and your chart plotter supports ARPA, then if you connect the two together the targets should pop up on your PC as soon as they are identified on the radar.

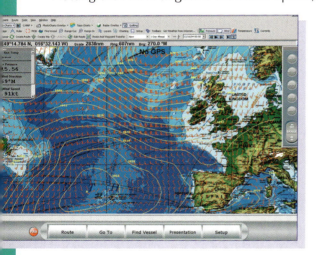

Getting a full radar overlay on the PC is a considerably more complex matter, and generally speaking, the chart plotting software will tie in to one specific radar manufacturer. Raymarine's RayTech obviously support their own radars, Nobeltec and Euronav have linked up with Koden, and MaxSea with Furuno. There are generic interface units from Nobeltec and Maris (for use with MaxSea), but they are relatively expensive and difficult to configure, so this is not a route I would recommend.

There is a fundamental difference between Koden's approach and that of Raymarine and MaxSea. With Koden, the radar scanner plugs directly into the computer through an interface box, and there is no need for a radar display. With MaxSea and RayTech, on the other hand, you need to have an electronic chart plotter/radar display, in addition to your PC. The Koden route is technically the neatest, and is also more cost effective. The others give you a backup with

NAVIGATION

the separate PC and electronic-based systems, and people will often mount the electronic unit in the cockpit as a waterproof deck system, but it is a more complex and expensive route.

Having the radar overlaid on the chart has a number of advantages. First, it gives a confirmation of the accuracy of your GPS – if the radar coastline diverges significantly from the chart, then you know that either the GPS is outputting an incorrect position (either due to a glitch in the GPS system or the failure of your equipment), or the horizontal chart datum is different from the WGS84 datum used by GPS. Most electronic charts are converted from the original paper datum to WGS84, but this is not guaranteed,

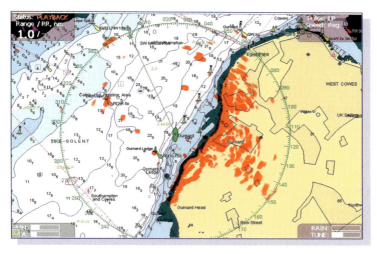

Nobeltec VNS with radar overlay.

especially if you go to out of the way places where the datum of the original paper chart is not known. If there is a GPS or chart datum problem, you can fix your position with the radar, taking a range and bearing on a known object, and from this you can determine any position offset that needs entering.

Having ARPA targets is useful with or without the full radar overlay. You can identify as a target any ship in the vicinity, and having it plotted on your chart allows you to see the ship's track and position

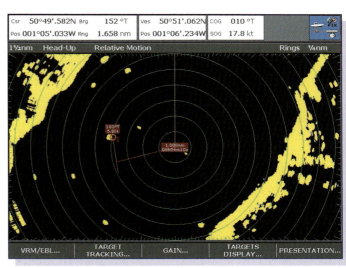

Raymarine radar, showing an ARPA target.

73

COMPUTERS ON BOARD

in relation to the chart, and from that to have a good idea where it is likely to be heading next. Also, as a position fixing aid, you can select a fixed object as an ARPA target, and then determine your position as a bearing and distance from this object – the more commercially-oriented chart plotters will allow you to use this as the means of fixing your position.

If you are combining your radar with your chart plotter to give a full radar overlay, it is worth having a large screen (with a minimum 15in display) so that it does not become too cluttered with information. Alternatively, if you are keeping the two separate, then mounting the radar and your PC screen side by side makes it very easy for the navigator to take in the information from both sources.

AIS

AIS (Automatic Identification System) is a unit carried by all ships that transmits over VHF the ship's details, position, course and speed, destination, call sign and so on. Each ship's unit also picks up AIS transmissions from other ships, and in coastal waters, shore-based vessel management systems will also pick them up.

Although the full AIS transceiver equipment is relatively expensive, lower cost, receive-only units are available, and connecting one of these up to a chart plotter or to a dedicated software package will give information on all vessels in the vicinity with AIS switched on. A Class B standard transceiver for smaller vessels is just about to hit the market, which sends less data at a slower update rate and over a shorter range, but will be significantly cheaper than the commercial Class A transceivers.

Even though AIS is advertised by some as a radar, it is really totally different. It gives a positive set of information about a vessel, but does rely on the AIS transmitter being switched on. In comparison, radar requires nothing of the targets it detects, but they may be land or ships, and you do need to interpret the radar image.

> **AIS is advertised by some as radar, but is totally different**

In terms of interfacing, the AIS messages are similar to, but not compatible with, NMEA, and so need to come in to the computer on a separate port. However, once this is done they will pop up on the screen in exactly the same way as ARPA targets, assuming the chart plotter software supports them. There is an issue of information management here, though. Because the AIS receives so much information, the software has to limit what is displayed on the screen, to keep it legible, and yet display all of the information from a given target when the need arises.

NAVIGATION

NAVIGATION UTILITIES

Many people still prefer a hybrid form of navigation, relying on GPS for position fixing, but then plotting the position on traditional paper charts (which everyone should carry, along with a hand-bearing compass and sextant, in case of electrical or GPS failure). For these, there

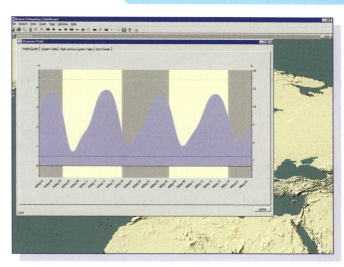

TideWizard: an easy to use height calculator.

are still a number of useful utility programs to make life easier. A popular example of this is tide height prediction software such as TideWizard, TidePlotter and Neptune Tides – though be aware that TidePlotter and Neptune Tides have limited coverage outside the British Isles, and TidePlotter only runs for 1 or 3 years from when purchased. Another product, for those going further offshore, is WinAstro, which performs all your sextant sight reduction calculations.

INTERFACING

The standard way of interfacing instruments to each other and to computers is via the NMEA0183 standard. This is essentially serial data, interfacing to the computer via a serial port. As these are now pretty rare on laptops, you will need a USB to serial converter. If you start running short of USB ports, you can add a USB hub, as described in the hardware chapter.

A new standard, NMEA2000,

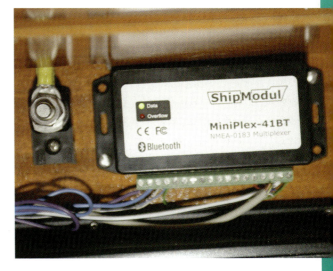

An NMEA multiplexer combines the NMEA outputs of several instruments.

COMPUTERS ON BOARD

also exists, offering much more robust communications, higher speeds (250kbps compared to 4.8kbps), cabling carrying power and data, and a single data network through the boat. This is quietly being adopted by manufacturers under their own brand names, such as Teleflex's MagicBus, Raymarine's ST290 and E series radars, Simrad, Lowrance, and engine manufacturers such as Volvo Penta, Evinrude and Yamaha. NMEA2000 is presently not supported by any PC software, though no doubt this will come in time. At the high end, the latest equipment from Raymarine and Furuno has adopted the standard TCP/IP network protocol – this just plugs into your PC's LAN port, for use with RayTech or Furuno's version of MaxSea.

Open standards such as NMEA are great for the end user, as well as for connecting instruments from different manufacturers. However, the electronic manufacturers often use their own proprietary protocols between their own instruments, citing better integration, but also tending to lock you in to one manufacturer's range of equipment. Luckily for the user, they generally have NMEA interfacing capabilities either built in or as a separate module. There is one application area where there is no open standard yet: radar. As discussed in the Radar/ARPA section, each manufacturer uses their own proprietary protocol, so PC software supporting radar overlays tends to be tied in to one manufacturer.

CHART PLOTTER COMPARISON

There are many PC-based chart plotters on the market, and this is inevitably confusing for potential buyers. To help clarify things, the main PC-based chart plotters available in the UK (excluding dedicated race packages) are summarised below, with particular strengths highlighted.

Admiralty RYA Chart Plotter

A budget package consisting of a folio of charts and basic chart plotting software. Charts

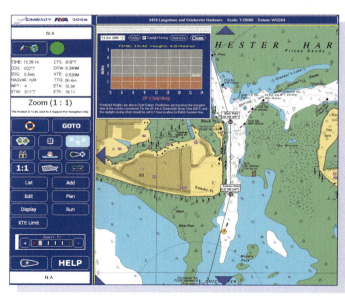

Admiralty RYA chart plotter.

are raster format, and folios only cover areas around the British Isles. The software receives data from your GPS, and now includes tide height and basic tidal stream calculations. Note also that the software requires the CD to be in your CD drive when running.

Imray Digital Charts

In many ways this product is similar to the Admiralty plotter, though using Imray charts instead of Admiralty. At present, chart folios are limited to the English Channel, southern North Sea and Brittany. The software does not have the Admiralty's tidal features, but can send routes and waypoints to your GPS.

Maptech Chart Navigator

As with the Admiralty RYA Chart Plotter and Imray products, the entry level Maptech Chart Navigator is bundled in with each chart folio. Maptech produce the official raster charts for US waters, and they also have reasonable coverage for much of Europe. The basic software is similar to the Imray and Admiralty products.

The Pro version of the software adds full interfacing to all of your instruments, including autopilot, AIS and ARPA; support for S-57 format charts in addition to Maptech; head up and North up chart displays; GRIB weather overlays; and display of tide heights and tidal streams (though no use of tidal streams in passage planning).

Software On Board (SOB)

DigiBOAT produce the SOB software for use with C-Map's NT and NT-Max vector charts. These offer excellent worldwide coverage, and are attractively priced. The basic Lite version of SOB is available free of charge, or you can upgrade to the full version for a very reasonable US$50, which gives you a lot of features for little outlay, so for the comparison we'll assume you have the full version.

SOB interfaces to all of your instruments, including autopilot, AIS and ARPA. One interesting feature is its anti-grounding tool, looking along your ground track and reporting on any nearby shallow water hazards. Of course, for this to give accurate information, you need to have the most detailed charts for the area. SOB will display the tides, but doesn't take them into account with navigation calculations.

seaPro

Euronav produce the seaPro range of chart plotters, and have a strong following in the UK. The starting point in their product range is seaPro Lite, which uses Euronav's own Livechart vector chart format for its charts (which offers good coverage throughout Europe). It offers an autopilot interface, and also displays tide height curves. As with other entry-level packages, it is bundled with a chart folio. SeaPro Lite Plus offers the same features as Lite, but also supports ARCS, BSB and S-57 chart formats.

COMPUTERS ON BOARD

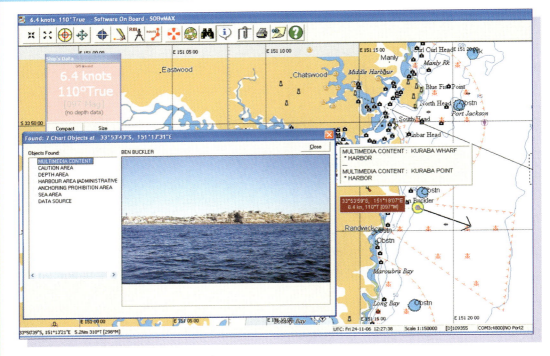

SOB chart plotter with C-Map NT/Max charts.

The standard version of seaPro is rightly popular with many British boaters. Its use of tidal streams in navigation is excellent, and it also includes GRIB weather overlays, basic polars and weather routing. Chart format coverage is as for seaPro Lite Plus, and vector charts can be viewed in 3D. It interfaces to all instruments, including ARPA and AIS receivers and offers full radar overlay, with Koden radars.

To help you get the most out of your sailing boat, there is the performance sailing module. This enhances the polar and weather routing tools (including automatic update of your polars), and adds features such as laylines on your chart, enhanced displays and graphs of your instrument data, calculation of the actual tidal stream and the geographical wind, output of data to your instrument displays, and race navigation tools.

MaxSea

MaxSea has long been a popular choice for blue water cruising and ocean racing sailors, though now the company seems to be concentrating on areas outside the leisure sector.

NAVIGATION

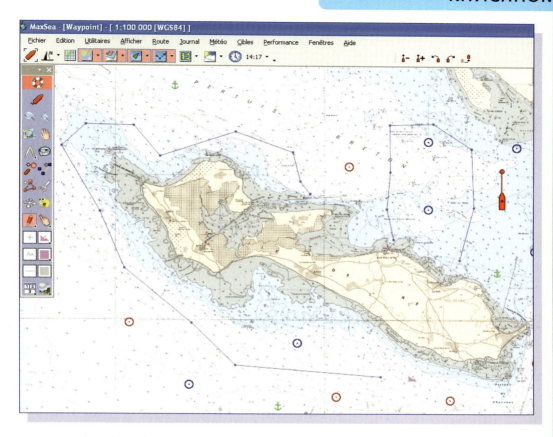

MaxSea chart plotter showing a planned route.

A strength of MaxSea has always been its support of multiple chart formats. For raster charts, it supports its own MapMedia charts, Maptech, UKHO ARCS charts, American Softchart, and Canadian NDI charts. For vector charts, it supports both C-Map and S-57 formats. Tidal stream atlases are also available, and if present allow for course to steer calculations. Weather is supported by GRIB files, and their Chopper tool to request GRIB files. Optional modules are available for weather routing (which is very good), a less useful performance sailing module, and AIS and ARPA interfacing.

If you have Furuno NavNet instruments, then the NavNet version of MaxSea makes interfacing to your instruments very easy. It also enables you to have the NavNet radar and fishfinder incorporated into MaxSea, assuming you have the electronics and the optional MaxSea modules.

The different permutations and combinations of MaxSea versions, supported chart formats and optional modules are quite complex, and I would recommend visiting a MaxSea specialist dealer to work out what you want.

COMPUTERS ON BOARD

Nobeltec

Nobeltec have long been the strongest US player in the PC navigation market, and are now entering the European market. They are owned by Jeppesen, who now also own C-Map, and Jeppesen are in turn owned by Boeing, so they have more resources than many companies in this industry.

Nobeltec Visual Navigation Suite.

There are two versions of their software: Visual Navigation Suite (VNS) as a mid-range product and Admiral for the top end. A common feature between both versions is the well designed, highly configurable user interface. Chart support is for their own Passport charts (which have worldwide vector charts, plus raster charts for specific areas, aerial photos, and high resolution 3D data), Maptech, S-57, and SoftChart and NDI charts. The VNS software will show the tides, and has basic tidal features in navigation planning. GRIB files can also be displayed for the weather. The software interfaces to all your instruments, including autopilot and AIS.

RADAR INTEGRATION

Nobeltec's radar integration is very good. The best option is their InSight radar scanner (developed in conjunction with Koden), that just plugs into your computer's network port. Unlike Raymarine and Furuno/MaxSea, Nobeltec's InSight doesn't need to have an electronic radar display as well. Both VNS and Admiral support radar, though Admiral also supports ARPA, and double speed rotation.

Alternatively, if you already have radar installed, the InSight BlackBox radar unit interfaces to many radars, to make the Nobeltec software a slave display of your radar, with all settings being made on the radar rather than through the computer.

NAVIGATION

The Admiral version refines a lot of the elements in VNS, and also adds support for many big boat features: multiple screens, networking across several computers, and the NavView user interface, designed for use with touch screens or pointing devices. For those wanting to enhance sailing performance, Nobeltec offers the Sailing Plus Pack. This supports polars and laylines, and also graphs trends of boat performance, wind and other parameters, although it doesn't include the use of polars in route planning or weather routing.

> **Nobeltec are now entering the European market, and have more resources than many**

RayTech

Raymarine's RayTech software is at its best when interfaced to Raymarine instruments. With the latest E-series, you just connect into the system with a single network cable, which carries instrument data, charts, radar and fishfinder. For earlier instruments, you need a seaTalk serial cable for instrument data and, if you want to share charts, radar and fishfinder, an HSB interface to your USB port (a PCMCIA version is also available, though not as reliable as the USB interface). The software also has an NMEA interface, for interfacing to other manufacturer's instruments.

Without the HSB interface, RayTech is just another mid range chart plotter, though interfacing to seaTalk instruments is very straightforward. It supports C-Map and Navionics vector charts, as well as Maptech raster charts. Tidal streams are displayed, but not used in calculations. GRIB files can be imported or downloaded through the Internet, and the software has comprehensive tools for polars, weather routing and sailboat performance built in. Add the HSB interface, and the software is fully integrated with your radar and chart plotter. Charts are read into the PC from the plotter, as well as giving you the ability to control and display your fishfinder and radar.

SUMMING UP

Chart plotters are now commonplace: the question is whether to go for a basic or an advanced one on your PC, a dedicated electronic one, or to stick with traditional means of navigation, perhaps aided by utilities on your PC. The next few years are going to be interesting, with developments in the supply of enhanced, intelligent information.

COMPUTERS ON BOARD

USEFUL WEB SITES

CHART PLOTTING SOFTWARE
ALIS – www.alismarine.co.uk
B&G – www.bandg.com/deckman.htm
DigiBOAT –www.DigiBOAT.com.au
Euronav – www.euronav.co.uk
Furuno – www.furuno.co.uk
Imray – www.imray.com
Koden – www.koden-electronics.co.jp
Lowrance – www.lowrance.com
Maptech – www.maptech-marine.com
MaxSea – www.MaxSea.com
Nobeltec – www.nobeltec.com
Simrad – www.simrad.com
Raymarine – www.raymarine.com
UKHO – www.admiraltyleisure.co.uk

ELECTRONIC CHARTS AND INFORMATION
C-Map – www.c-map.co.uk
Navionics – www.navionics.co.uk
(see also Euronav, Maptech, MaxSea, Nobeltec and UKHO)

WATERPROOF SCREENS
KS Bootronik – www.bootronik.de
Raymarine – www.raymarine.com

NAVIGATION UTILITIES
Belfield (for TidePlotter) – www.tideplotter.co.uk
Neptune – www.neptune-navigation.com
Smartcom Software (for WinAstro and TideWizard) – www.smartcomsoftware.com

NMEA INTERFACING
Autonnic Research – www.autonnic.com
Marine IQ – www.marineiq.com
Tinley Electronics – www.tinleyelectronics.com
Teleflex – www.teleflexmarine.com

ENTERTAINMENT

ENTERTAINMENT

Whether it's for you, or something to keep the kids quiet, there will be some form of entertainment on board. The question is, how much do you want to do on the computer? Computer-based entertainment systems have developed tremendously over the last few years, but as always there are pros and cons.

The benefits include saving space (by having everything in one box or on your hard disk, there is no hunting for CDs) and the ability to edit digital photos or video, which can only be done on a computer. The drawback is that computer-based systems are often not as easy to use as dedicated units, and the quality is not as good (though whether you notice this in a yacht environment is debatable).

COMPUTERS ON BOARD

This chapter looks at CDs and DVDs, radio and TV, digital photos and videos, and how to spread things round your boat. Although the focus is on PC-based systems, equivalent solutions are generally available for the Mac.

SOUND

Of course your computer can play CDs, but it can also play MP3 files (or similar). For those who don't know, these are highly compressed audio files (at best 128kbps, as opposed to 1411kbps for uncompressed audio). There is some loss of audio quality, though when played through an MP3 player the playback and headphones are generally of a standard that you don't notice this.

MP3 players can share sound tracks with your PC.

There are some alternatives to the MP3 format, such as Microsoft's Windows Media Audio (WMA) format, though these are not as ubiquitous as the MP3 format. On a computer, the big advantage is that you can easily fit all your CD collection onto your hard disk – to do this, just insert your CD, start up the latest version of Windows Media Player, and select *Rip*. In a few minutes, your CD will be copied to your hard disk. No more hunting for that missing CD!

As well as playing audio that you already have on board, if you have Wi-Fi, you can also access Internet radio. Most stations are broadcast either in Windows Media Player format, or in RealPlayer format, so it is worth making sure you have both of these programs on your PC. If you know what you want to listen to, you can generally find it on the radio station's web site. Alternatively you can go to one of the listings pages, such as www.live-radio.net

There are also some computer-based radio receivers. Some are FM receivers, such as those from Griffin Technologies, or if you

ENTERTAINMENT

also want LW and Weatherfax you may use ICOM's PCR-1500 or WiNRADiO's WR-G33EM.

Of course, you may want to keep your entertainment separate, but still be able to hear the audio output **You can easily fit all your CDs onto your hard disk** from your PC on board. Rather than fitting an extra set of speakers just for this, or relying on your laptop's tinny speakers, you can easily connect the audio from your PC to the boat's entertainment system.

VISION

If you are using your PC for video, there is a benefit in using Windows XP Media Centre Edition. This offers a large format user interface as an alternative to the standard Windows one, geared towards entertainment use, and includes

Windows Media Centre PCs are often smaller and more stylish than standard machines.

enhanced tools for viewing photos, DVDs, CDs, TV and radio. It also comes with a TV-style remote control.

Your PC will almost definitely play DVDs, so do you need a separate DVD player? It depends on whether or not someone will want to watch a DVD whilst you pick up your e-mails, or plan tomorrow's trip. If the answer is yes, keep them separate.

Windows Media Centre adds on features for home entertainment.

Similarly, having the TV tuner in the PC means that you can record broadcasts to the hard disk to replay later, or pause live TV, but you can't use the PC for anything else, and it must be running. Alternatively, you can replace the computer screen with a flat screen TV that takes PC input as well, so you can watch TV independently of the PC. If you go abroad, though, standards raise their ugly head. Most of Europe uses PAL as its TV standard, of which there are some six versions, but most modern TVs will cope with all of these. France uses its own SECAM system, and whilst most French TVs will support PAL and SECAM, not all non-French TVs support SECAM. Finally, if you plan to go to the Americas, NTSC is generally used, and few TV tuners support both PAL and NTSC – you are better off with an external TV tuner that you swap over mid Atlantic.

COMPUTERS ON BOARD

As at home, the TV can display both standard and Freeview TV (with a suitable Freeview tuner). And, thanks to the EU, all of Europe uses the same DVB-T standard, so your Freeview tuner will also pick up similar broadcasts where available. This is increasing – between 2007 and 2012 we will see all analogue TV channels in Europe switched off.

But local TV will always be in the local language. What if you want English language TV? Then you need a satellite receiver, to pick up Sky. The key thing here is dish size. A 40cm diameter dish, whilst initially attractive, will only cover from the North Sea down to the south coast of France. Increasing to a 60cm diameter dish gives you all of the British Isles and the Med from the Adriatic westwards.

Unlike your domestic satellite dish, you can point the dish to different satellites, to pick up other broadcasts – standards permitting! Sky uses its own proprietary format, unlike the rest of Europe, so to receive those other stations you need a separate decoder box. And if you go to the US, as well as needing another decoder, you also need to change the LNB in the satellite dish.

HARDWARE

If you are using your computer on the entertainment side, there are some additional hardware factors to take into account, to avoid computer noise interfering with your enjoyment and to keep it user friendly. Using a laptop, you don't have much choice, but if you are going for a built-in PC then you do have some control.

Noise Reduction

Cooling fans are the biggest source of noise, and they will sound a lot louder on your boat than in the computer showroom. Some power supplies are designed to have quiet fans, and the processor and graphics chips also feature quiet fans and heat sinks. There are also the clicks and whirrs from your hard disk. Some are quieter than others, but you can buy a sound insulating enclosure for it. Keeping the computer in a locker is a great way of muffling noise, though it needs good ventilation for cooling. Also, bear in mind that a higher spec PC or a smaller case generally means more cooling air needs pumping round, which means more fan noise. Some computers are designed specifically for use with media applications, and these have a great deal of attention paid to noise reduction. It is well worth investing in one of these. To take things further, pay a visit to one of the web sites specialising in this area, such as www.quietpc.co.uk.

> **The cooling fans are the biggest source of noise**

ENTERTAINMENT

Access

If you will be using the CD/DVD drive for a lot more than just installing programs, you need to make sure that it is easily accessible. Alternatively, if you cannot easily access your drive, you can fit an external one in a more accessible location on a USB cable.

Connecting

When connecting things up, remember that, in general, the audio and video connections can be kept separate. This is particularly useful when it comes to TV and DVD, as the speakers built into most flat screen TVs are not nearly as good as those in your radio/CD player. Putting the audio through the radio/CD player generally gives a much higher quality, clearer sound.

S-Video uses a 4 pin Mini-DIN connector.

The audio output from a PC is not amplified, so you either need to put it through an amplifier, or use active speakers (which all PC speakers are) – these are just speakers with a built-in amplifier. If your entertainment system has a spare auxiliary input, you can simply connect to this. Otherwise, an easy solution is to fit an FM modulator. This sits between your FM antenna and your radio, and is connected to the audio output of your PC. Tune your radio to the frequency of the modulator (normally settable by DIP switches), and you will hear your computer's audio.

RCA video connector.

Different connector types carry different quality signals

On the video front, the key thing to bear in mind is that different connector types are not just physically different, they also carry different quality signals. At the bottom of the heap is the RCA push-on connector, carrying composite video. Next, there is the S-Video signal with its Mini-DIN connector. And best of all there is RGB, with separate cables for the red, green and blue colours. Most devices now also support SCART connections. The connector

SCART connectors can be used for RGB or S-Video.

COMPUTERS ON BOARD

supports input and output of both RGB and S-Video (as well as stereo audio), though only one of the two can be used at a time. Also, be aware that not all SCART cables connect all pins in the connector, and that the SCART sockets in the equipment may not support all of SCART's capabilities. So, to get the best result, try and use the best quality video signals, and if using SCART check what is actually supported.

USEFUL WEB SITES

COMPUTER RADIO RECEIVERS
Griffin Technology – www.griffintechnology.com
ICOM – www.icomuk.co.uk
WinRadio – www.winradio.com

TV SYSTEMS
DVB – www.dvb.org
Freeview – www.freeview.co.uk
KVH – www.kvh.com
Seatel – www.seatel.com
Sky – www.sky.com

QUIET PCS
Acousti Products – www.acoustiproducts.com
Quiet PC – www.quietpc.co.uk
Zalman – www.zalman.co.kr

AUDIO/VIDEO CONNECTION ITEMS
CPC – www.cpc.co.uk
Keene Electronics – www.keene.co.uk
Lektropacks – www.lektropacks.co.uk
Maplins – www.maplins.com

PUTTING IT ALL TOGETHER

PUTTING IT ALL TOGETHER

Here are a number of typical systems that have been put together for different sizes and types of boat. The diagrams are schematic, and should not be taken to be detailed wiring diagrams. Rather, this chapter is intended to help you focus your mind on what you want to have installed on your boat, in terms of both hardware and software.

COMPUTERS ON BOARD

E-MAIL ALONGSIDE

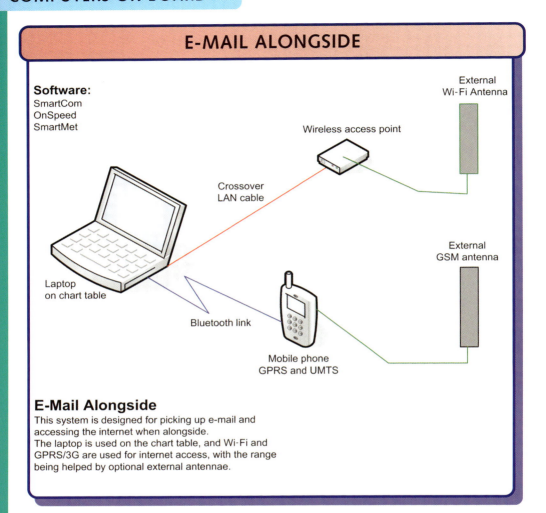

Software:
SmartCom
OnSpeed
SmartMet

External Wi-Fi Antenna

Wireless access point

Crossover LAN cable

External GSM antenna

Laptop on chart table

Bluetooth link

Mobile phone GPRS and UMTS

E-Mail Alongside
This system is designed for picking up e-mail and accessing the internet when alongside.
The laptop is used on the chart table, and Wi-Fi and GPRS/3G are used for internet access, with the range being helped by optional external antennae.

PUTTING IT ALL TOGETHER

COASTAL SAILING CRUISER

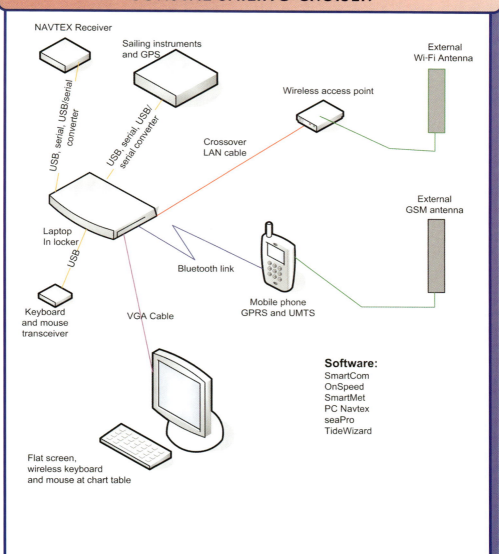

Software:
SmartCom
OnSpeed
SmartMet
PC Navtex
seaPro
TideWizard

Coastal Sailing Cruiser
A system for a typical coastal sailing cruiser using the computer for navigation and communications.
Adding to the comms, seaPro is used for its tidal stream handling, and PC Navtex brings NAVTEX messages onto the PC.

COMPUTERS ON BOARD

COASTAL RACER

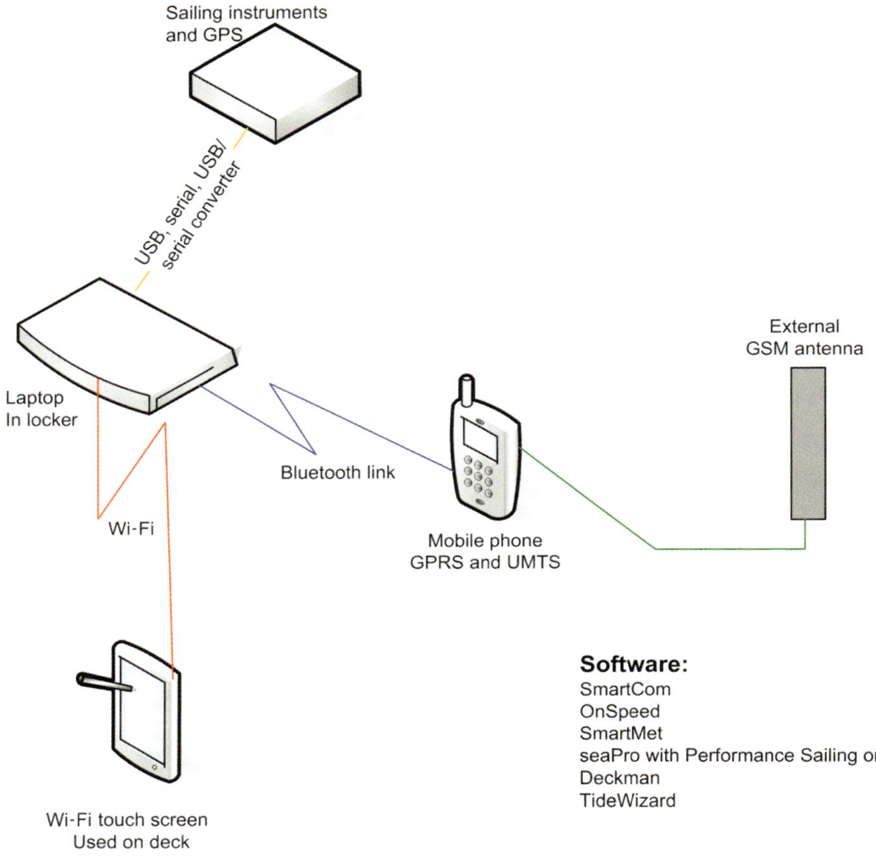

Sailing instruments and GPS

USB, serial, USB/serial converter

Laptop
In locker

External GSM antenna

Bluetooth link

Wi-Fi

Mobile phone
GPRS and UMTS

Software:
SmartCom
OnSpeed
SmartMet
seaPro with Performance Sailing or Deckman
TideWizard

Wi-Fi touch screen
Used on deck

Coastal Racer
The wirelesss screen lets the navigator carry out all his work on the rail. The system has just the essential requirements for racing, with non-essential items omitted to save weight and windage

PUTTING IT ALL TOGETHER

POWERBOAT WITH RADAR AND ENTERTAINMENT

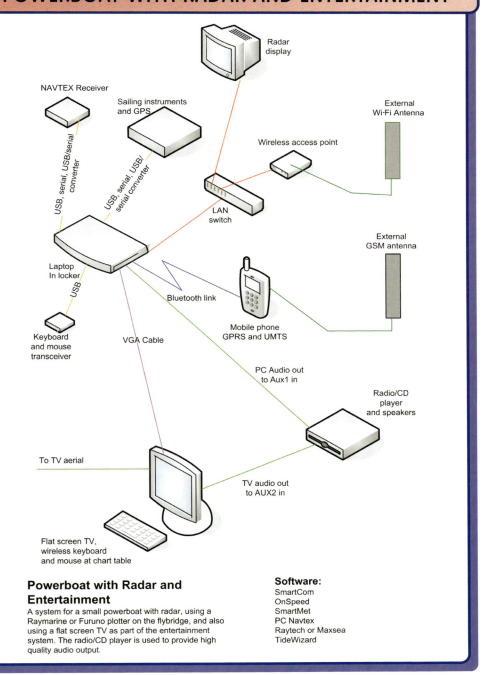

Powerboat with Radar and Entertainment

A system for a small powerboat with radar, using a Raymarine or Furuno plotter on the flybridge, and also using a flat screen TV as part of the entertainment system. The radio/CD player is used to provide high quality audio output.

Software:
SmartCom
OnSpeed
SmartMet
PC Navtex
Raytech or Maxsea
TideWizard

COMPUTERS ON BOARD

OCEAN CRUISER SYSTEM

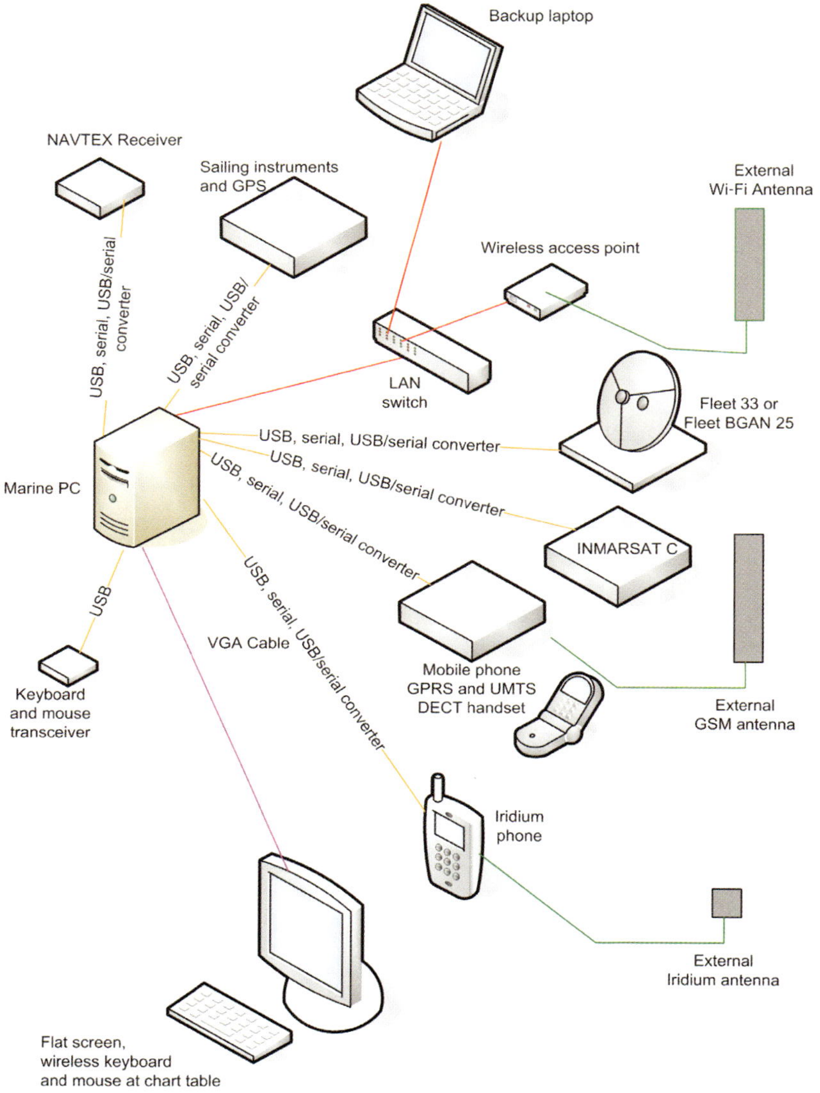

Backup laptop

NAVTEX Receiver

Sailing instruments and GPS

External Wi-Fi Antenna

Wireless access point

USB, serial, USB/serial converter

USB, serial, USB/serial converter

LAN switch

Fleet 33 or Fleet BGAN 25

Marine PC

USB, serial, USB/serial converter

USB, serial, USB/serial converter

USB, serial, USB/serial converter

INMARSAT C

USB, serial, USB/serial converter

USB

VGA Cable

Mobile phone
GPRS and UMTS
DECT handset

External GSM antenna

Keyboard and mouse transceiver

Iridium phone

External Iridium antenna

Flat screen, wireless keyboard and mouse at chart table

Ocean Cruiser System
This shows the navigation and communications systems for a well equipped ocean-going yacht. Radar and entertainment may be added in as well if required.

Software:
SmartCom
MailASail
SmartMet
PC Navtex
PC SatC
seaPro or Maxsea
TideWizard

PUTTING IT ALL TOGETHER

LARGE YACHT SYSTEM – NAVIGATION

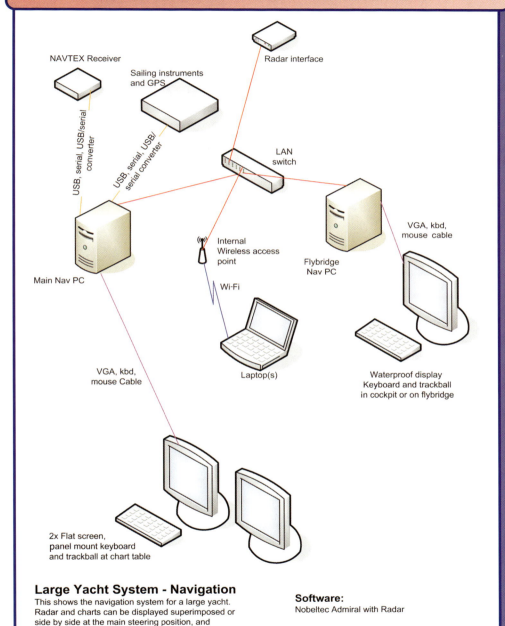

Large Yacht System - Navigation
This shows the navigation system for a large yacht. Radar and charts can be displayed superimposed or side by side at the main steering position, and independently on the flybridge or on laptops on the internal Wi-Fi LAN.

Software:
Nobeltec Admiral with Radar

COMPUTERS ON BOARD

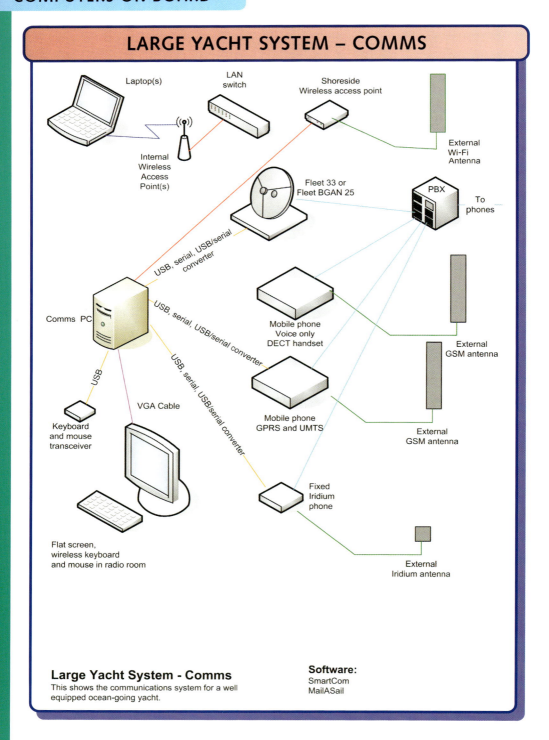

OVER THE HORIZON

There are a number of interesting developments coming up over the next few years, and this chapter will look at the direction things are moving in. As always with crystal ball gazing, not everything below will actually materialise, and there is bound to be some new technology popping up that we have not foreseen. To give this some structure, we'll follow the sequence of the book's chapters.

COMPUTERS ON BOARD

COMPUTER HARDWARE

Computers continue to get faster, and this increases their power requirements. Although Windows Vista will require a step up in processor power, computer power continues to exceed what is needed on board. We may see a move towards marine PCs with lower power processors, probably coming from the industrial PC sector. These will be a longer term investment, more resistant against heat, humidity and vibration, and running off the boat's DC power supply.

It may be possible to buy off the shelf computer systems, with everything pre-installed and ready to go. This is already the norm with navigation systems installed on large yachts and commercial vessels, and will percolate down so that the computer is installed as a standard component in the boat, rather than an afterthought.

COMMUNICATIONS

There is already a communications divide between PCs in the home or office running off broadband, and those on the move looking for Wi-Fi (and when this isn't available, taking resource in GPRS or satellite phones). Increasingly, operating systems and applications software will be written with the assumption that the user has broadband access. This could end up with a dedicated PC on board, using software designed without the need for broadband, supplemented by a laptop for use at home or with Wi-Fi when available.

WiMAX will probably be rolled out in the marinas in the near future – if only because its greater range makes it easier to give good coverage in the marina. A side effect of the greater range is that people will have access within a few miles of the marina, from nearby moorings and anchorages. Rather than trying to block them, as occurs in some marinas at the moment, the marina operators will probably start charging a premium for those who want large downloads.

Mobile phone companies will roll out new models, with better comms. These will include Wi-Fi as well as GSM/GPRS/3G, though the operators will no doubt try to charge for the use of Wi-Fi for voice and data. We will also see HSDPA being rolled out to replace 3G, giving download speeds of about 1Mbit/s, and then HSUPA as the next generation. However, coverage of these new technologies is likely to be localised, as at present the number of users of 3G data communications (as opposed to owners of phones with those capabilities) has stopped increasing.

OVER THE HORIZON

WEATHER

We can see the continuing trend away from sources like Weatherfax, and towards Internet delivery. As well as making access easier, it will also allow access to higher resolution forecasts, as provided by the likes of Theyr, WindGuru and SmartMet.

Stepping back to the wider picture of GMDSS, the current system has been unchanged for about 30 years now, and discussions are beginning about possible replacements. This will probably follow the route of using the Internet, which was not available when GMDSS was first developed.

NAVIGATION

The basics of electronic navigation are well established now, and we will see a continuing move from traditional to electronic navigation. One aspect of this is the increasing use of e-navigation, where, instead of laying expensive physical navigation marks, virtual navigation marks will be laid using systems such as AIS.

Another forthcoming event is that of the rise of GNSS, the collective acronym for GPS, Galileo and the Russian Glonass. We will soon see multi-standard receivers, which will be more robust than GPS receivers. They will also be more accurate, but it must be remembered that in most parts of the world, any standard GPS receiver is more accurate than the charts, so higher accuracy is a red herring for normal navigation.

> **Virtual navigation marks will be laid using systems such as AIS**

There will also be an increasing consolidation of the producers of electronic navigation data and software – we are already seeing the beginning of this, with Furuno having taken a stake in MaxSea, and Jeppesen having bought up both Nobeltec and C-Map.

Charts will develop from the split between raster and vector into hybrid charts, where the clear display of raster charts is combined with an underlying, intelligent database. With the way raster charts are produced these days, it is easy to split the chart up into layers, giving them much of the flexibility of vector charts.

We can also see the electronic navigation data extending from charts to all of the data needed by the user – sailing instructions, almanac data, mooring information and shore-side facilities. With increasing communications bandwidth

COMPUTERS ON BOARD

in coastal waters, we can envisage this being delivered over the Internet, either in its entirety or for real time updating of data supplied on CD.

ENTERTAINMENT

Entertainment is steadily going digital, and with the increasing bandwidth of Internet connections we will soon see useable TV over the web – most of the existing TV companies are already experimenting with this. If you just want to get TV when you are in a marina, you will probably be able to see your TV programs over the Internet, rather than needing a satellite TV system.

For on-board entertainment systems, we will increasingly see UPnP (Universal Plug and Play) devices: computers and entertainment systems hardware can be plugged together to give audio and video round the boat. We are already seeing some manufacturers producing UPnP systems, as Windows software or as dedicated media servers or players.

Still related to entertainment, there will also be greater possibilities for shoreside monitoring and control of your boat. Many producers of GSM or satellite-based tracking devices will warn you if your boat moves out of a given area, or allow you to track its position via the Internet. This can be extended to viewing your boat through a webcam, and to having alarms for events such as low batteries, bilge water and so on.

SHUTDOWN

With the computer being such a general tool, it can be put to a myriad of uses. The question you have to ask yourself is what do you want to do on the computer, and what do you want to do using dedicated electronics, or even not do at all.

COMPUTERS ON BOARD

The one thing that the computer is essential for is the Internet, and this has probably been the biggest driving force in getting computers onto boats. As we have seen, this way of communicating has its pitfalls, but hopefully this book has steered you round them. The way computers can receive and display weather information is persuading an increasing number of users to discover the attractions of on-demand, detailed weather forecasts delivered via the Internet.

The other big driver is navigation, and the computer can navigate more intelligently than an electronic plotter. Whether you want this, or prefer to use an electronic plotter, or even (dare one say it) paper charts, is really down to your preferences.

On the entertainment side, things are not as clear cut, and it really boils down to personal preference. There is little unique about having a PC-based entertainment system, though it does reduce the number of pieces of equipment on board.

There is no single ideal computer system for use on board, but I hope that you now know some of the things to consider when deciding what is right for you and how you will use it, as well as some of the things to take into account when setting the system up. Now just get out there and enjoy yourself!

JARGON BUSTER

AIS: Automatic Identification System. Ships use this service to broadcast their position, route etc over VHF radio in a digital format, which can be received and plotted on some chart plotters

AMD: a rival to Intel, producing PC processor chips

ARPA: Automatic Radar Plotting Aid. The plotting and tracking of targets on a radar

AVG: A manufacturer of anti-virus software

Backplane: the base board on a computer, into which expansion boards are plugged. On most PCs the backplane has the CPU, RAM and other chips incorporated onto it. In many marine and industrial PCs a passive backplane is used, which has minimal functionality, and into which a processor board is plugged

CAT5: Category 5 standard network cabling

Composite video: the analogue TV image signal, carried down a single co-axial cable

COM port: a serial port on a PC, normally taking a DB-9 9 pin serial connector, though sometimes taking a 25 pin DB-25 connector (which is functionally identical)

CPU: Central Processor Unit. This is the 'brains' behind your computer, doing all the calculations

DDR: a computer memory standard. Double Data Rate Synchronous Dynamic Random Access Memory in full. Current PCs use DDR2, with older machines using DDR (also known as DDR1), and DDR3 is under development

DECT: Digital Enhanced Cordless Telecommunications. The standard for digital cordless phones, with a range of up to 100 metres from the base station in open air

DIP Switch: compact slider or rocker switches, generally mounted in a block

DNS: Domain Name Server. A server on the Internet that converts between domain names (eg www.google.com) and IP addresses (eg 123.234.123.234)

COMPUTERS ON BOARD

FCT: Fixed Cellular Terminal. The 'engine' of a GSM phone, with connections to a PC and a phone or PBX, used for installing fixed GSM phones on board

GB: Gigabyte. Measure of the amount of memory in the computer, and hard disk capacity

GFS: Global Forecast System. The US world weather forecast model

GPRS: General Packet Radio Service. A fast mobile data service, precursor to 3G

Graphics Processor: a separate processor in the computer, for generating the screen display

GRIB: GRIdded Binary. A file format for the exchange of weather forecast data

GSM: the most common mobile phone standard, named after *Groupe Spécial Mobile*, the EU body who selected the protocol

3GSM: a generic term for mobile phone data connections that are faster than GPRS

HSB: Raymarine's high speed data bus for sharing radar, fishfinder and chart data between devices. The original HSB bus was based on ARCNET, a 2.5Mbps industrial network protocol. This has now been supplanted by the faster HSB2 bus, based on Ethernet technology

HSDPA: High Speed Downlink Packet Access. The next step on from 3GSM

HTML: Hyper Text Markup Language. A file format for formatted documents, initially for web pages and now widely used in e-mail

IP: Internet Protocol. The component of TCP/IP responsible for routing data between computers

ISDN: Integrated Services Digital Network. A standard for digital voice and data over the telephone network, used by Inmarsat Fleet 55 and 77 to give a guaranteed speed connection, used for tasks such as video conferencing

ISP: Internet Service Provider. A company or organisation providing users with access to the Internet

KVM: Keyboard, Video and Mouse. Generally referring to switching or sharing of screens, keyboards and mice between PCs

LNB: Low-Noise Block converter. On a satellite dish, this receives the high frequency signals from the satellite, amplifies them and converts them to a lower frequency, so they can be sent through normal co-ax cable

Mesoscale: a high resolution weather forecast, with more accurate physics than synoptic forecasts

JARGON BUSTER

Mini-DIN: 9.5mm diameter, smaller version of DIN connectors, with variable numbers of pins

MPDS: Mobile Packet Data Service. The packet data service used on Inmarsat Fleet satellites

MP3: MPEG-1 Audio Layer 3, the *de facto* compressed audio format for computers and portable players

NMEA0183: the most common standard for interfacing of marine electronics

NMEA2000: a replacement standard to NMEA0183, slowly gaining in popularity

NMEA Sentence: a set of data used by the NMEA0183 protocol, eg $IIR00,3,12,34,5 defines a route of three waypoints, going from waypoint 12 to 34 to 5

PAL: Phase-Alternating Line. A standard for colour TV transmission, used in Europe (except France), the Middle and Far East, Australasia, and much of Africa and South America

PBX: Private Branch exchange. A phone exchange fitted in the office or on board, allowing multiple phone handsets to access multiple external lines (which may be landline, mobile or satellite phones)

PC Card: a credit card sized expansion card for laptops, most commonly used for GSM data cards. Now being replaced by USB devices

PCMCIA: now renamed PC Card (see above)

PDA: Personal Digital Assistant

PDF: Portable Document Format. A common file format for documents, created using Adobe Acrobat

Phono Connector: an alternative name for an RCA connector

POP: Post Office Protocol. Used to receive e-mails. A POP server on the Internet holds all the e-mails for your e-mail address, until you log on and download them to your computer

PS/2: a connector type used for keyboards and mice. Previously a version of PC produced by IBM

RAM: Random Access Memory. The memory in your computer

Raster: a chart that is an image, identical to a paper chart, eg ARCS, Imray, Maptech or Mapmedia

RCA Connector: a jack plug whose design was introduced by the Radio Corporation of America

RGB: Red, Green, Blue. A video signal split into its three component parts

RTF: Rich Text Format. A format for text files with fonts, colours etc, now largely replaced by HTML

RTTY: Radio TeleTYpe – sending text messages over radio

SafetyNET: weather forecasts and navigation warnings broadcast over Inmarsat C

SCART: an audio/video connector developed by the *Syndicat des Constructeurs d'Appareils Radiorécepteurs et Téléviseurs*

COMPUTERS ON BOARD

SIM: Subscriber Identity Module. A smartcard used in all GSM and many satellite phones to store information such as the user's phone number and network details

SIP: Session Initialisation Protocol. How Internet phone calls are initiated and terminated

SMS: Short Message Service, or text messages, on mobile phones

SMTP: Simple Mail Transfer Protocol, used to send e-mails from your computer out to the Internet, via an SMTP server on the Internet

SSB: Single Side Band, generally referring to an MF/HF marine radio

Synoptic: a low resolution, global weather forecast model

S-Video: Separate Video, where brightness and colour are carried on two separate wires

SYNOP: surface synoptic weather observations, encoded in WMO code FM-12, giving current weather reports

TCP: Transmission Control Protocol. The component of TCP/IP that enables the exchange of data between programs, so that they can communicate

TFT: Thin-Film Transistor. A liquid crystal display technology where each pixel has its own transistor switch on the screen. Used for almost all LCD displays

USB: Universal Serial Bus. Fast becoming the standard interface for computers

VESA: Video Electronics Standards Association. A body that produces many video standards for computer displays, varying from electronic interface specifications to screen mounting dimensions

VMG: Velocity Made Good. The component of a vessel's speed in a specific direction, generally either to the next waypoint or (for sailing boats) to windward

VoIP: Voice over IP. Sending voice over the Internet, eg for phone calls

Webmail: reading your e-mail through a web browser such as Internet Explorer

Wi-Fi: Wireless LAN. Short range (up to 100m), high speed Internet connectivity over radio

WiMAX: a high speed, long range version of Wi-Fi

WMA: Windows Media Audio, Microsoft's audio compression format

WW3: WaveWatch3. The oceanographic forecast model operated by the US Navy, and used by many forecast services

Vector: a chart that is drawn from a database, eg C-Map, Livechart, Navionics and Passport, S-57

INDEX

Page numbers referring to diagrams or illustrations are set in italic type.

3D views 63
3GSM 26, 27, 28, 37, 98

ACeS 19
Ad-Aware 49
AIS 63, 74, 77, 78, 79, 99
ALIS 67
AMD 3
antenna 18
anti-virus software 27, 46–7
AOL 36, 39
Apollo 2 31
ARCS 77, 79
ARPA 63, 72–4, 77, 78, 79
AT&T 36
authenticated SMTP 40

BGAN 15, 26
Bluetooth 12
Bonito 54
broadband 15, 25, 26, 98
BSB 77

C-Map 63, 77, 79, 80, 81
cable 11, 18, 87
CD 84
chart plotter 62ff

Combitech 54
compression 26
CompuServe 36, 39
cooling 6, 86
course to steer 64
CPU 3, 10, 92

Deckman 60, 63, 68,
DECT phone 17, 22
dial-up modem 25
DigiBOAT *see* SOB
display 4
Domain Name Server (DNS) *36, 37*–8
DVB-T 86
DVD 85

e-mail 38–42
e-navigation 99
Euronav *see* seaPro

FCT 17, *18*
firewall 47–9
fixed PC 6
Fleet 26, 28, 30, 37
FM Modulator 87
Freeview 86

Furuno 63, 64, 72, 79

GFS 59
Globalstar *19*, *20*, 26
Global Marine 59
Gmail 39
GMDSS 99
GNSS 99
GPRS 25, 26, 28, 37, 98
GPS 73, 99
graphics processor 10
GRIB files 59, 63, 71, 77, 78, 79, 80
GSM 17, 25, 30, 36, 98

Hotmail 39
HSB 81
HSDPA 26, 27, 98
HSPA 27, 98
HTML 41

ICOM 85
IMAP 38–9
Imray 77
industrial PC 6
Inmarsat *19*, *20*, 26
Inmarsat C 53

COMPUTERS ON BOARD

installation 6
Intel 3
Internet Explorer 38
internet radio 84
Internet Service Provider (ISP) 35–8, *36*, 40, 47
internet TV 100
inverter 9
Iridium 19, 20, 23, 26, 31, 36
ISDN 30

keyboard 6
Koden 72, 78, 80
KVM 7, *8*

laptop 5, 6
Linux 1
Livechart 77

Mac 1
MailASail 28–30, 32–3, 39
Mapmedia 79
Maptech 77, 79, 80, 81
MaxSea 59, 60, 63, 64, 67, 71, 72, 78–9
memory 3, 10
mini-M 26, 36
mouse 6
moving weather 59
MP3 84
MPDS 26, 30, 37

Navimail 59
Navionics 63, 81
NAVTEX 52–3
NDI 79, 80
Neptune Tides 75
network 8, 9
NMEA 12, 66, 72, 75–6
Nobeltec 63, 64, 67, 68, 71, 72, 80–1
noise 86
NTSC 85

OCENS 59
OnSpeed 28–30, 31
Outlook 39, 41–2, 45

PAL 85
Passport 80

passive backplane 6
PBX 21, *22*
PC NAVTEX 52–3
PC SatC 53
PDA 5
performance 4
Pipex 36
plain text 41
PocketMet 60
polars 69, 78
POP 38–9
power consumption 10
power supply 6, 9, 10

radar 63, 72–4, 80
RAM 3
raster charts 66, 99
Raymarine 59, 63, 64, 71, 72, 81
RealPlayer 84
remote display 7
repair 7
Rich Text Format (RTF) 41
roaming 18, 27
routes 66
RS232 port 11

S-57 77, 79, 80
SafetyNET 53
Saildocs 59
sailing performance 68–9, 78
satellite TV 86
screen 4, 10
seaPro 60, 62, 67, 68, 77
SeaTalk 81
SECAM 85
serial port 11
SIM card 17, 19, 28, 36
Sky 86
Skype 16, 27
Slipstream 31
SmartCom 28–30, 31–2, 39, 43–6
SmartMet 59, 99
SMS 19
SMTP 38–9, 40, 43–4, 47
SOB 62, 77
Softchart 79, 80
spam 40, 48
spyware 49

SSB radio 54
systems 90–6

TCP/IP 44, 76
text messaging 19
Thuraya 19, *20*, 26, 36
tides 64, 67, 75, 77, 79, 80
TidePlotter 75
TideWizard 75
Toughbook 5
TV 85–6

UKHO 62, 76–7
UPnP 100
USB port 11, 12, 75–6
UUPlus 28–30, 33

vector charts 66, 99
VESA 4
video signals 87–8
Vista 5, 92
VMG 70
Voice over IP (VoIP) 15, 16

warranty 7
waterproof display 4
waypoints 66
weather routing 71–2, 78
weather web sites 55–8
Weatherfax 54–5
web browsing 38
web mail 39
Wi-Fi 5, 8, 9, 12, 15, 22, 25, 27, 37, 98
WiMAX 17, 25, 98
Windows 1, 5
Windows Messenger 27, 42
Windows Update 27
WMA 84
WW3 59

Xaxero 54
XP 5
XP Media Centre Edition 85

zap 28–30, 33